THE OTHER SIDE OF LEADERSHIP

RECLAIMING POWER AND PURPOSE ON
YOUR LEADERSHIP JOURNEY

BY BRANDISS T. PEARSON, ED.D., FNP-C

DEDICATION

For Shaun, my quiet flame.

For Brandon, my joyful fire.

I am braver and better because of you.

Thank you both!

Love, Mommy

CONTENTS

PREFACE 5

THE BECOMING

01. Camryn's Story: The Empty Seat 8

02. Camryn's Story: The Hidden Frame 15

03. Camryn's Story: The Mirror of Change.........................22

04. Camryn's Story: Curating Confidence 33

05. Camryn's Story: The Mic and the Moment................42

06. Camryn's Story: No Seat At The Table 50

THE UNLEARNING

07. Camryn's Story: The Weight of the Blazer 60

08. Camryn's Story: The Bench Under the Oak Tree.........67

09. Camryn's Story: The Door Without a Handle 74

10. Camryn's Story: The Pebbles and the Jar 84

THE RISING

11. Camryn's Story: Rising Strong.................................91

12. Camryn's Story: The Exit That Saved Her 100

13. Camryn's Story: Not Starting From Scratch 111

14. Camryn's Story: When It Finally Feels Right.............123

CLOSING: BECOMING NEVER ENDS 136

PREFACE

OPENING LETTER:
"YOU DON'T NEED PERMISSION,
BUT I'M GIVING IT ANYWAY"

Dear Leader,

If you're reading this guide, I already know something sacred about you:

You're becoming.

You're showing up in rooms that don't always feel built for you.

You're wrestling with doubt while carrying brilliance. You're leading anyway.

I wrote this for the woman I used to be, the one pretending in boardrooms, shrinking in silence, and second-guessing every sentence that came out of her mouth. The one who had the title but didn't yet believe she had the *right* to be there. The one who wore straight hair to interviews, hid her paintings of powerful Black images during Zoom calls, and worried that being fully herself might cost her everything.

Maybe that woman is you right now.

If so, I want to be to you what I never had:

A hand to hold.

A mirror that reflects your magic.

A voice whispering, *"Come with me. I've got you."*

Here's the truth: No one ever gave me a blueprint for leading as a woman from the margins. No one taught me how to bridge the space between poverty and power, between invisibility and impact. I had to write it as I walked it, step by trembling step.

This is that blueprint.

It's not polished. It's not perfect. It's not linear.

But it's real. It's hard-won. And it's yours now.

Inside, you'll find stories, strategies, and practices that helped me go from hiding to healing, from performing to leading, from doubting to becoming.

You'll learn how I moved my body to reclaim it.

How I gave fear a front-row seat and still did the thing.

How I started saying no to opportunities that didn't align.

How I began speaking what I sought until I saw it in my life, my circle, and my reflection.

Most importantly, you'll be reminded that you don't have to earn your *enoughness*. You already are.

So take what you need. Leave what you don't. Come back when you're weary.

This blueprint is living and breathing, just like you.

You don't need permission to rise. But if you've been waiting for someone to say:

"You belong here. You're allowed to be all of who you are. You're not alone."

Let me be the first.

You've got this, and I've got you.

With love,

Brandiss

PART

One

THE BECOMING

CHAPTER 1
CAMRYN'S STORY:
THE EMPTY SEAT

Camryn adjusted the hem of her navy blazer for the fourth time, fingertips brushing the edge like it might unravel if she didn't hold it in place. The fabric was smooth but stiff, new, like her title, like this room. Her seat at the long mahogany table came with no manual, just pressure. Her palms were already clammy, her notepad still blank inside her leather folio. The boardroom buzzed with the sound of confident familiarity: laughter that came easy, business chatter delivered like rhythm and blues with a cadence only the seasoned seemed to know.

She sat halfway between the window and the door, a little too far from the power center but not quite invisible. Her eyes darted toward the heavy glass walls framing the room. They reminded her of church windows, beautiful, transparent, and just enough to make her feel caged.

Camryn J. Morgan, Director of Strategic Initiatives.

The nameplate was a declaration. Her name was crisp in black font. It was real. It was earned. It just hadn't settled into her skin yet.

She smoothed her skirt over her knees and adjusted her posture. She wore her grandmother's pearl necklace and earrings to boost her confidence. Her nails were perfectly manicured in a neutral shade, strong, rounded, deliberate. Her coils were shaped into a soft halo, not a single curl out of place. She had moisturized with her homemade honey-almond-shea butter blend that morning, and it mingled with the faint notes of coffee, toner ink, and air-conditioned ambition. She looked like she belonged here. And still, she squirmed in her seat in an attempt to find a comfortable posture.

"They said I belonged here," she whispered to herself, her voice barely audible under the clinking of coffee mugs and shifting chairs. "So why do I feel like I need permission to speak?"

The room was cool. Too cool. Designed for wool suits and high-stakes negotiations. The scent of lemon floor cleaner lingered beneath the more expensive notes of someone's Oud cologne. Camryn's hands rested lightly on her leather folio. Inside, she had color-coded notes, backup stats, and a brilliant campaign idea. She was ready. Absolutely ready. And yet, her heart tapped against her ribcage like a warning knock.

A senior VP at the far end of the table dropped a joke about quarterly projections and budget approvals. Laughter followed, easy and full of shared history. Camryn nodded even though she hadn't caught the joke, too distracted by the war happening inside her. She smiled reflexively, the way you do when you're at a cookout full of relatives you've never met but don't want to offend.

Speak up.

Not yet.

Say something.

Don't say the wrong thing.

Smile. Look engaged.

Don't look too eager.

She scribbled into her notepad, the pen gliding over the paper:

Add value. Speak soon. Don't mess this up.

She had practiced what to say the night before, alone in her bedroom, standing in front of her bathroom mirror, rehearsing variations of "I agree" and "To build on that..."

But now, seated in this sterile, echoing space filled with practiced voices and confident gestures, her own voice felt buried under layers of self-doubt.

Here, under recessed lights and behind expensive eyeglasses, her voice felt buried beneath protocol and performance.

Across the table, someone brought up the campaign strategy, *her* campaign strategy. This was her chance. She leaned in. Opened her mouth.

"To build on that," she had said aloud. "Let me offer another lens…"

She was immediately interrupted by a rumble of voices from two seats down. A man. Older, louder, less *melanated*.

He spoke as if he owned the very oxygen the people in the room were inhaling.

She eased back slowly, the cool leather chair swallowing her resolve. Her gaze drifted to the empty seat beside her. It was untouched, no laptop, no jacket. A void. She imagined it being reserved for someone like her. Someone Black. Someone brilliant. Someone who was expected to sit and soak up strategy rather than contribute to it. It mocked her with its vacancy. Was it reserved for someone who didn't show up? Or someone who, like her, had once shown up and never truly arrived?

Around the room, the discussion continued without her contribution. More acronyms. More banter.

She glanced at the framed DEI statement on the wall, in bold font and muted colors. It stared back like a promise deferred. "Diversity, Equity & Inclusion!" She chuckled inwardly, not from humor, but from the bitter irony. She was the diversity. The checkbox. The "fresh perspective" that had not yet been asked for a single perspective.

"Thanks for being here, Camryn," someone said as the meeting ended.

Not, "Excellent point."

Not, "Well said."

Just… thanks. For showing up. Quietly.

She inhaled deeply. Her scent, the light scent of honey, almond, and shea wrapped around her like a whisper of who she truly was: a woman not new to brilliance, just new to this space.

As the chairs scraped back and the room emptied, she sat still, fingers grazing the cool edge of the table. Her hands trembled slightly from the overstimulation of the moments before. She pressed her palms flat against the glossy surface and steadied herself, almost as if marking territory.

She glanced over at the empty seat once more. She imagined it filled with her insecurities. Her past shame, guilt, and failures. Then, she interrupted those thoughts and imagined replacing the negativity with affirmations about her own resilience, grit, and fortitude.

What would it have looked like to speak up today? To offer her brilliance before it was requested? To double down when she was interrupted?

She didn't know. Not yet.

But she knew that she brought clarity, knowledge, and vision forged in years of preparation to this space.

Back in her apartment that night, Camryn slowly and intentionally made her way through her nightly self-care ritual: lighting her favorite scented candles, playing soft music, and immersing herself in a hot bath while reading her favorite urban fiction novel.

After climbing out of the bathtub, she completed her skin care routine and gathered her hair into her silk bonnet. She sat on the edge of her bed and looked up at the wall where her diploma hung above the mounds of pillows.

She reached for the journal on her nightstand, grabbed the pen she always left next to the journal in case inspiration struck in the middle of the night, opened it to the available empty page, and wrote:

I am not here to decorate the room. I am here to reshape it.

The next morning, she arrived early. This time, the chatter in the boardroom didn't feel so suffocating. It felt like a blank canvas. And when the conversation once again landed on campaign strategy,

Camryn didn't wait. Her voice was warm. Intentional. Rooted. Heads turned. Someone wrote something down.

She subtly glanced over at the empty chair beside her and smiled as she thought to herself, "mission accomplished."

AUTHOR'S REFLECTION: FROM SILENT SPACES TO SELF-AUTHORITY

I didn't walk into leadership.

I stumbled. I tiptoed. I performed.

My first leadership role wasn't a grand arrival.

It felt like a setup, like someone needed a face that checked a box, and mine happened to be convenient that day.

I had the title, but not the voice. The seat at the table, but not the script. The proximity to power, but no real preparation.

No one ever taught me how to transition from surviving to leading. No one told me how to go from "Make it out" to "Make it count."

And when you come from poverty, real poverty, you don't just carry your own insecurity.

You carry the ghosts of everyone who never made it out. You carry questions like:

- Am I just lucky?
- Am I supposed to speak up here?
- Do I even belong?

I didn't know what executive presence looked like, at least not in a body like mine. I hadn't seen leadership modeled in a way that felt accessible, or even possible, for a girl like me.

So I watched. I mimicked. I code-switched. I smiled more than I spoke.

I didn't want to mess up the opportunity, but I also didn't know how to fully take up space.

That's what imposter syndrome *really* feels like:

It's not just self-doubt.

It's the deep, unspoken fear that your presence is conditional.

That, if you stop performing, if you show up as your whole self, the doors might close just as quickly as they opened.

So, I dimmed.

And I survived that way, for a while.

But survival is not leadership.

It's not thriving.

It's not freedom.

And I was meant for freedom.

REFLECTION PROMPT FOR THE READER:

Think of a space where you've been present, but silent.

Where have you performed instead of participated?

_____

_____

_____

_____

What have you internalized about what leaders "should" look or sound like?

_____

_____

_____

_____

Who told you that you couldn't lead exactly as you are?

_____

_____

_____

_____

CHAPTER 2
CAMRYN'S STORY: THE HIDDEN FRAME

Camryn hovered over the **"Start Video"** button on Zoom, the softclick pressure of the trackpad beneath her fingertip.

For the third time that week, she whispered an apology to no one and hit **"Off."**

Bandwidth issues, she would type in the chat, again. The lie heavy on her fingertips as she typed the words.

She leaned back in her upholstered desk chair and exhaled through parted lips, warm breath stirring the faint scent of peppermint tea that had gone cold beside her keyboard. Behind her, the painting filled most of the wall: thick, textured strokes of saffron, indigo, and crimson, a riot of color against the neutral gray apartment paint. A Black woman haloed in unapologetic coils donned with a bright gold crown, chin tilted skyward with a confidence in her eyes, lips parted in an almost smile, and hoop earrings shimmering with quiet cultural pride. The canvas radiated heat, like sunbaked streets after summer rain.

Camryn first saw the piece at a Harlem street fair. She recalled the moment she saw the painting. She had spent the summer interning at a Fortune 500 company in Upper Manhattan, but commuted from her Brownstone in Harlem. One weekend, she decided to explore the culture-rich streets of the neighborhood she called home for those 12 weeks of summer. That day, the air was thick with the scents of halal meat and roasted corn mingled with diesel fumes from the food trucks. The rumble of loud reggae basslines, car horns, and the vibration from the passing subway train below the street created a syncopated rhythm that was true to the culture of the neighborhood. The sounds and smells were as anchored to the community as the people who lived there.

As Camryn strolled by one of the vendors along 125th Street, her eyes landed on the painting. The artist, who had their massive locs tucked into a vibrant scarf, and a gap-toothed grin as wide as freedom, had spoken low and soft:

"She's a mirror, sis. She'll show you who you *are*, not who you pretend to be."

Camryn bought the painting on the spot. It had followed her like a faithful elder, from a five-story walk-up Brownstone in Harlem to a shoebox apartment in Midtown Atlanta, a steady presence during each relocation, promotion, heartbreak, and rebirth. A silent witness to her becoming. Now it stared at her from the tidy corner of her home office, watching her hide behind "bandwidth issues."

She angled the webcam up until only a blank eggshell wall filled the frame. Safe. Neutral. Sterile as a hospital sheet.

She tugged at her roots, her real roots. Since ditching the chemical relaxers, her thick coils had bloomed, dense and springy, smelling faintly of coconut oil and rosemary water. She loved the way they felt, velvety under her palm, but every Monday she still coaxed them into a low bun, slicked her edges into submission with gel that dried tight on her scalp.

Professional, she told herself.

Palatable was the truth.

On her desk, the white pages of her pastel pink planner glared up at her: back-to-back directors' briefings, an executive town hall, a DEI roundtable she was "invited" to at the last minute, an afterthought with a calendar link. She'd be visible this week, her video tile in every virtual room.

Visible, but not real.

Lately, she felt like a hologram, present yet translucent. Bright but muted. She cloaked curves under boxy cardigans, softened her sentences with question marks, and thanked people for interrupting her mid-idea, to keep the peace. She learned to exist subtly like fragrance, there but not touchable. She took up space like a whisper, afraid that volume might equal violence in someone else's eyes.

Her phone buzzed against the desk: a chime reminding her of the 3:00 p.m. team call. Camryn stood, smoothing the satiny blouse that skimmed her torso. The airconditioner clicked on; a cool breeze blew across the bare parts of her arms, carrying a faint note of eucalyptus from her scented oil diffuser.

She moved toward the painting. Under afternoon light, the woman's painted coils glistened, and the gold hoops caught flecks of sun. Camryn felt like the woman in the portrait stared back at her. The painted woman wasn't begging for approval. She was *testifying*.

Camryn's throat tightened.

She returned to her desk and stared at her own reflection in Zoom's video preview: loose curls escaping that overworked bun, pecan-tan skin glowing against a rosegold ring light, a hesitant smile tugging one corner of her mouth. She didn't look unprofessional. She looked … like herself.

She inhaled, notes of honey, almond, and shea from her body butter mingling with the earthy coffee she just poured, still steaming in her mug, and clicked the camera **on**.

The painting blazed behind her like a sunrise no one could dim.

Little squares populated the screen, polished faces framed by tidy shelves, white shiplap walls, and succulents in clay planters. Camryn braced herself for a gasp or a polite *Oh!* from a box in the top row. But no one blinked; no one side-eyed. They dove straight into project updates, performance dashboards, and itemized deliverables.

Camryn listened; fingers poised on her keyboard. When her turn came, she unmuted, pulse thrumming in her ears like bass booming at a concert. She offered a concise analysis, a steady cadence, and no quicksand qualifiers like *'just'* or *'maybe.'* Her voice carried a warm timbre. It didn't crack. She didn't shrink. She spoke once and then fell silent, letting her words breathe without apology.

Forty-two minutes later, the meeting ended. Before she could close the window, an alert pinged. **New Message.**

"Hey… just wanted to say I saw your painting. It's stunning. Felt like a breath of fresh air. I've been nervous to bring my whole self to this job, but seeing you today reminded me that maybe I don't have to hide."

Camryn's vision blurred. She blinked, salty warmth gathering at her lashes. She looked back at the painting. The woman in the portrait seemed to nod, as if to say, *"**Told you**."*

Her fingertips grazed a single coil near her temple, the way her mother's hand used to rest there when nerves rattled her before spelling bees or job interviews. She remembered the first time teenage Camryn asked if her hair was "too much."

Her mom had laughed, low and light, accent seasoned by southern soil.

"Too much for who? Baby, your hair is a crown. Some folks just haven't seen royalty."

Camryn closed her laptop. The metallic *clack* echoed in the quiet room like a gavel.

That evening, she didn't straighten her hair. She didn't have to move the painting back into its rightful space on the wall, because it was already there. She brewed ginger-cinnamon tea, sweetened it with a splash of oat milk, and let the spicy steam warm her face. She turned on a playlist of oldschool soul, horns sashaying through the speakers, and let the music wrap around her like a silk robe.

Bare-faced, coiled, and radiant, she grabbed her journal from her bedroom nightstand and curled into the reading nook she created beneath the painting. She opened the journal, the pages ready to absorb confession. The pen slid across paper, ink flowing like a river bursting its banks:

"I have spent so long perfecting professionalism that I have exiled presence.

Today, I let presence lead, and the ground did not swallow me.

Today, I was both art and artist.

Maybe power begins the moment I refuse to dim."

She paused, listening to the soft tick of the wall clock, the muted city sounds drifting through an open window, laughter from a balcony upstairs, a distant siren, and the metallic squeal of the MARTA brakes. Life layering itself, unfiltered.

Camryn set the journal down and touched the canvas, thick ridges of acrylic under her fingertips. She could almost feel the artist's heartbeat left in each stroke, the promise that standing whole might free someone else to do the same.

Tomorrow, she knew she would be on camera again. Tomorrow, questions might come, the curious, the careless, the coded. But tonight, soulful horns melted into twilight, and a painted woman kept watch.

Camryn whispered, "Thank you," to the canvas, to the artist, to the courage that finally loosened its wings.

AUTHOR'S REFLECTION: THE DAY I STOPPED HIDING MYSELF TO MAKE OTHERS COMFORTABLE

There's a particular kind of exhaustion that comes from constantly editing yourself.

Not just your emails or your résumé, but your face, your voice, your hair, your walls.

During COVID, like many of us, I found myself on camera more than ever. And every time I prepared for a Zoom meeting or virtual interview, I did the same thing Camryn did.

I would move my paintings out of view.

Paintings of Black women, bold, beautiful, defiant, free.

Paintings that looked like me.

Paintings that reminded me of where I came from and who I was becoming.

But I hid them. Because I had internalized the lie that my identity was "too much" for professionalism. That braids weren't boardroom. That Black art wasn't executive decor. That authenticity was a liability.

I kept my hair straight for interviews.

I kept my speech soft and my stories surface-level. I played the part.

Until one day, I didn't.

There wasn't a grand speech or a major protest.

There was just a quiet decision: *I want to see myself while I lead.*

I started leaving my paintings up.

I started wearing my hair the way I felt most like myself, sometimes straight, sometimes coiled, sometimes braided.

I stopped styling myself to soothe someone else's bias.

It was subtle at first.

But then something radical began to happen:

I stopped trembling when I spoke.

I started hearing myself in full voice.

And more importantly, *others* started hearing me too.

That's the irony.

When I finally stopped hiding to fit in,

I started to *belong*, not to the system, but to myself.

Why does this even matter?

Because authenticity isn't just personal, it's political.

Every time a woman of color brings her whole self into a space that wasn't designed for her, she redefines what leadership looks like.

Representation isn't just about being visible. It's about being *whole* while visible.

That shift? That's where the power lives.

REFLECTION PROMPT FOR THE READER:

What parts of yourself have you been hiding to feel more "professional?"

_____

_____

_____

_____

What would it feel like to bring those parts into the light?

_____

_____

_____

_____

What's your version of leaving the paintings in view?

_____

_____

_____

_____

CHAPTER 3
CAMRYN'S STORY: THE MIRROR OF CHANGE

Camryn wiped a crescent of dust from the antique mirror with the inside edge of her sleeve, releasing a faint scent of attic musk. The aroma of dry cedar, sunbaked cardboard, and something sweet, yet stale, like forgotten perfume. The glass beneath her swipe revealed a dusty, smudged reflection and, for a blink, two versions of herself: one shadowed by grime, the other sharpening into focus. She squared her shoulders. The mirror was heavier than she remembered, as if the decades of family history trapped in its wood had fattened it. The gold trim, once bright, now wore jagged freckles of tarnish; the carved corners of small roses and twisting vines now had chipped petals. Heat warped the once-strong oak frame, but the piece still stood proud, tilted against the wall, as if waiting, patient as the ancestors.

She rediscovered the mirror last month while helping her mother clear the attic of their small family home, a space that smelled of insulation dust and fading triumphs. The mirror had huddled behind baby blanket boxes, tarnished track medals, and lopsided shoeboxes stuffed with grade school report cards and certificates she had earned throughout her school days.

When Camryn peeled back the old curtains, now yellowed from years of UV rays, the light sliced through the window and kissed the mirrored glass, and for a moment, she'd felt something flutter in her chest, recognition maybe, or something even more profound.

"You want that old thing?" her mother had asked, arching a brow while balancing a tote of holiday décor on her hip.

Camryn simply nodded, throat tight. She couldn't articulate why, only that the mirror pulsed like an extra heartbeat in her chest.

Now, late evening lamplight skimmed across her bedroom's eggshell walls and haloed the mirror in an amber glow. Camryn stood barefoot on cool wooden floorboards, arms folded, cardigan sleeves resting on her forearms. Her apartment still smelled of tonight's dinner. Roasted garlic, sweet paprika, the buttery finish of purposely lumpy homemade mashed potatoes, but the air near the mirror felt different, tinged with lavender oil from the diffuser she kept for restless nights.

She expected revelation, maybe judgment. Instead, the reflection staring back looked... weary. Not from lack of sleep, though she was learning that six hours and ambition seldom mixed, but from a deeper weariness; the weight of performing excellence in every room she stepped into. She studied the soft hollows beneath her cocoa-brown eyes. Her capable shoulders, sculpted from morning push-ups and years of carrying family hopes, rose and fell in a slow, deliberate breath. Her body was there, capable and shaped by resilience, but it felt foreign, like a satin suit tailored for someone else, an outfit she was still getting used to.

She adjusted her stance, grounding her toes against the polished wood; the reflection mimicked. Her hair freshly styled, falling in jetblack spirals to her collarbones, glistened. She'd always loved the spicy earth aroma of the bergamot oil her stylist used, the way it perfumed the air when she turned her head.

Then something strange happened.

The mirrored Camryn smiled first, soft and knowing.

Tiny dimples appeared on either side of her mouth.

Camryn's eyebrows twitched.

"Hello," the reflection said. No sound, yet the words reverberated inside her chest like a low drumline. "I'm you. Just... further along."

Camryn's pulse thrummed in her ears, a bassline of disbelief. She swallowed the metallic tang of surprise. "You're in my head," she muttered, voice husky from disuse.

"I've always been," the mirror replied. "But now you're finally listening."

Lamplight flickered on the nightstand, and Camryn suddenly felt the room's hush, only distant city traffic and the faint tick-tock of her wall clock. It sounded like destiny counting beats.

For the first time in years, she slid down to the floor, cool boards pressing into the backs of her thighs, legs folded, palms resting atop kneecaps. She stared. No filter. No Zoom ring light. No LinkedIn headline. Just the drum of her heartbeat and the hum of refrigerator coils carrying midnight's hush.

She didn't flinch as she looked at her reflection in the mirror.

"I'm the version of you that knows her worth," the reflection continued. "The one who stopped hustling for belonging and started building from wholeness."

She stared at herself for what felt like hours. No filter. No prep. No audience.

In the days that followed, Camryn's time in the mirror became part of her daily routine. The grayish-pink light of dawn seeped through lacy curtains, and Camryn padded over sleepy floorboards to stand barefoot before her reflection.

Every morning, she stood in front of it. Sometimes she spoke affirmations, even if her voice cracked. Sometimes she stretched, letting her body remember that it was still hers.

She'd whisper simple, yet meaningful words like *"I love you, Cam,"* or *"Peace over performance."*

Sometimes she rolled her shoulders until they cracked softly and said, *"This body is not an afterthought."*

On particularly tender mornings, she let tears blur her view of the glass, swiping salty, wet, tear-drenched fingers across the dust she still hadn't entirely wiped away. The mirror never scolded; it only reflected.

Evenings, after spreadsheets, small talk, and microaggressions disguised as mentorship, she returned, not for performance but for presence. Some nights, she could almost taste fatigue. She would spend time slowing her mind. She'd watched herself breathe until her jaws unclenched and her shoulders dropped from her ears.

She began to notice the tiny betrayals: how her jaw hardened when she forced a polite laugh; how her shoulders rolled inward when credit for her idea slid across the table to someone louder; how her eyes dulled at clothes she had chosen in an effort to disappear instead of taking up space. Those were the moments she felt most defeated.

Inspired by her time in the mirror, Camryn decided to begin reclaiming herself by intentionally tapping into her five senses.

Sight.

Camryn placed a bouquet of marigolds on her nightstand, their citrus petals loud against white linen. She replaced harsh overhead lighting with a warm Edison bulb that bronzed her skin instead of bleaching it. She draped the mirror in fairy lights that glimmered like a softspoken crown.

Sound.

She curated a playlist, Erykah Badu's velvet croon, Nina Simone's thunder, a sprinkle of Afrobeats bass, a medley of soulful gospel hymns. Each morning she let those rhythms thread through her veins before emails or headlines could.

Smell.

Camryn blended vanilla and sweet almond oils, massaged them into her palms until the air smelled like sweet earth meeting sunrise. She lined the drawers with sachets of dried lavender to remind her of the future in which rest is rebellion.

Taste.

She rose early enough to taste life: tangy bursts of grapefruit, bitter espresso balanced by honey, toasted Ezekiel bread that filled the apartment with notes of warmth and goodness.

Touch.

She traded stiff pencil skirts for fabrics that sighed against her skin, satin tops, and wide-leg trousers that draped like reassurance. She moisturized elbows, knees, and dreams with whipped shea until both skin and spirit glowed.

Camryn stopped setting 5:00 a.m. alarms to race productivity gurus; instead, she greeted dawn slowly. Steam spiraled from the shower as she waited for the water to get "good and hot," as her mother used to say, fogging the mirror. She traced affirmations in the condensation: *"Chosen." "Capable." "Whole."*

Walks became opportunities for quiet worship as she played some of her favorite old-school gospel through her headphones. Asphalt radiated heat through the soles of her sneakers; the aroma of fresh-brewed espresso from the neighborhood coffee shop mingled with the scent of dogwood trees and cut grass. She occasionally turned the music off and tuned in to the sounds of her surroundings. She listened to her breath and footsteps orchestrating a private symphony. She thoughtfully considered moments of gratitude as she walked.

When she arrived back at home, she would sometimes put off showering to grab her journal and jot down inspiration before the fleeting thoughts left her heart and mind. Ink would flow quickly across the empty pages. Not bullet lists, but rambling pages brimming with confessions and revelations, with gratitude and prayers.

Sometimes her thoughts resulted in shorter bursts of inspirational messages and mantras, ones she made up, ones she borrowed, ones that felt like truth wrapped in language.

Sticky notes bloomed: saffron squares on the fridge, lime ones on her laptop, and lavender on the bathroom mirror. Mini love letters reading:

"Softness is strategy."

"I am the table and the feast."

"My presence upgrades the rooms I enter ."

"I am becoming, even when no one is watching."

"My softness is not weakness. It's wisdom."

"I don't need to hustle for a seat; I am the table."

Always, she returned to the oak-framed mirror in her bedroom, string lights flickering gold. It became a safe space, the hush between inhale and exhale, between imposter and embodied.

One evening, after a marathon of meetings that left her voice paper-thin, she slipped into the apartment and locked the door against the city's clang. The hallway light buzzed overhead. She kicked off patent pumps; relief moved from her arches to her calves as she peeled the cardigan from her shoulders. Satin camisole clung to her skin, still warm from stress.

The apartment's silence rang in her ears. She strolled over to the mirror, her tired, moist feet leaving a warm imprint on the cool floor. Her reflection greeted her, eyes rimmed in fatigue yet glinting like river stones. She looked different; not polished, not perfect, but *present*. A single coil broke free from her ponytail, brushing her cheekbone. She let it.

The mirror version of Camryn who was further along, lifted her chin and smiled, teeth bright as the moon. Camryn mirrored the motion, small at first, then radiant.

"You're catching up," the reflection whispered, voice velvet-deep. *"You're remembering."*

And she was.

Not overnight. Not in some grand transformation moment.

Not by miracle, but by a mosaic of daily practices: sunrise tea, shea butter sheened skin, stories spilled onto notebook lines, and playlists that pulsed like ancestral drums.

In boundary-setting texts and prayers whispered into the dark. In the decision to befriend her body. In the refusal to shrink.

No longer did she need the mirror to confirm her existence. But she still stood before it, not for permission, but for practice. Becoming wasn't a finish line; it was a series of moments with meaning, a trinity of inhale>exhale>trust. A rhythm. A remembering. A return to herself.

Camryn traced the edge of the frame, fingertips catching on a nub of chipped gold leaf, and thanked the mirror for holding both her reflection and her becoming. Then she turned toward her bed, the scent of lavender lingering like a lullaby. Outside, the city murmured itself to sleep.

Inside, she finally rested, whole, unhidden, and on purpose.

AUTHOR'S REFLECTION: JOURNAL ENTRY – I SAT WITH MYSELF TODAY

I sat with myself today. I have practiced mindfulness and sitting quietly in the past. I write in my journal regularly, pray daily, and encourage others to do the same, but today, I *sat with MYSELF!* I set a chair in front of my mirror in my bedroom, set a timer for five minutes, put my phone on "do not disturb," shut out all distractions, and stared myself in the eyes. I set my intention to focus solely on Brandiss.

Within moments, the tears began to flow freely down my cheeks. I hadn't *seen* myself in quite some time. The first thing I noticed was an almost overwhelming feeling of discomfort. I didn't want to *see* me. I wasn't sure what I would find. There are parts of me that I don't even allow myself to acknowledge. Shame, guilt, fear and insecurities were all on display as I looked myself in the eyes.

As tears fell, I took a deep breath and whispered, "I love you." It was almost as if I waited my whole adult life to say that out loud, and actually mean it. Not while in a ball gown with perfectly coiffed hair and my face buried under layers of makeup. In that moment, free of adornments, in my most natural state, I said, "I love you." I repeated it until I believed it. The tears were replaced with a smile as I allowed my eyes to move up and down, scanning my reflection. I noticed every imperfection. Each moment of discomfort was met with an affirmation of self-love. I've earned each scar in the battle of life and plan to wear them with honor.

Just as I noticed myself sitting up straighter in my seat, my chest poked out ever so slightly with an unearthed confidence, the timer began to chime. It startled me and thrust me back into reality. I silenced the alarm, looked back at the mirror, and whispered one more "I love you." Before leaving my seat, I took one more deep breath and said, "I'll see you tomorrow."

BUILDING AND BECOMING

I didn't just wake up one day confident.

I *built* her.

Brick by brick.

Habit by habit.

Because here's the truth no one tells you:

Imposter syndrome doesn't disappear with a promotion.

It just finds new ways to whisper.

You have to actively, *intentionally*, drown it out, with truth, with action, with care.

So I started building a life that could hold the weight of my becoming.

Not a hustle life.

A *healing* life.

And it started with the body.

I Moved to Remember

Leadership lives in the body.

I had to reconnect to mine, not just as a machine that got things done, but as a sacred vessel carrying wisdom, grief, intuition, and power.

I started moving.

Walking. Stretching. Breathing deeply.

Even when I didn't feel like it.

Not to lose weight. Not for aesthetics.

But to **wake myself up.**

Every time I moved, I remembered: *I am here. I am alive. I am worthy of this space.*

I Got Still to Hear Myself

I started scheduling silence.

Massages. Quiet time.

Time in the mirror with no filter, no titles, no to-do list.

Just me and the woman I was becoming.

I didn't always like what I saw.

But I stopped avoiding her.

I started *seeing* her, tired, resilient, divine.

And little by little, the tension in my shoulders loosened.

My thoughts slowed. My inner voice got clearer.

The noise of performance gave way to the music of purpose.

I Fed My Mind Like It Was Starving

I devoured books like *Atomic Habits*, *Lead From the Outside*, *The Alchemist*, *Purpose Awakening*, *You Are a Badass*, and *The Purpose Driven Life…*

Each one lit a different part of me on fire.

Not because they had all the answers, but because they reminded me that growth was a choice.

Every page reminded me: *I get to redesign my life. And I'm not crazy for wanting more.*

I Spoke What I Sought

I created mantras.

I said them out loud, yes, even when they felt fake.

"I am called. I am capable. I am chosen."

"My voice changes rooms, even when it trembles."

"I don't chase opportunity. I attract alignment."

I began to **speak what I sought** until I started to **see what I said**, in myself, in my circle, and in every space I chose to enter.

I Got Selective With My Yes

One of the most powerful rituals I built was the ritual of **discernment.**

Early on, I said yes to every opportunity out of fear:

- Fear of being forgotten
- Fear of seeming ungrateful
- Fear that this was "my one shot."

But eventually, I realized:

Every yes has a cost.

So I started asking different questions:

- Does this align with my personal mission?
- Will this nourish me or just drain me?
- Am I being invited because of my value, or because I'm safe for the system?

I began saying no without guilt.

And in doing so, I made room for **divine yeses**.

Routines Don't Make You a Leader, They Remind You That You Already Are.

These weren't productivity hacks.

They were soul contracts.

Practices that kept me anchored while the winds of doubt blew hard and often.

This is what it looks like to design a life you don't have to escape from.

This is what it looks like to lead without losing yourself.

REFLECTION PROMPT FOR THE READER:

What rituals or routines have you built, or need to build, to stay grounded in who you are becoming?

_____

_____

_____

_____

What's one practice you can begin this week to connect back to yourself?

_____

_____

_____

_____

What "yes" do you need to revoke to make room for your alignment?

_____

_____

_____

_____

CHAPTER 4
CAMRYN'S STORY: CURATING CONFIDENCE

The hotel conference center buzzed with a kind of energy Camryn didn't trust.

It was the kind that looked like networking and smelled like anxiety masked in designer perfume. The room was cold and sterile, with high ceilings, lit by chandeliers that bounced off glass water pitchers and silver platters of croissants nobody touched. Women in sharply tailored suits floated through the space like they'd rehearsed this dance a thousand times. Laughter flowed in predictable bursts. Lanyards gleamed like medals. Business cards passed like currency. Camryn watched the exchange like someone peering into a world she hadn't yet been invited to join.

She stood near the back wall, fingers wrapped around a lukewarm cup of hotel coffee; too bitter and too thin, but something to hold. Her other hand clutched her phone like a shield, thumb hovering over a text thread she wasn't reading. Her name tag read "Camryn J. Morgan, Director of Strategic Initiatives," but it felt more like a question than a credential. Like someone had typed it by mistake, and no one had figured it out yet.

She caught her reflection in the tall windowpane near the exit. Her lipstick intact, blouse crisp, posture practiced. But her voice? Her certainty? Her sense of safety?

Nowhere to be found.

There was a time when she would've blamed herself for that. But now, she knew better. This feeling wasn't about personal failure. It was about proximity. About walking into rooms never designed for you and trying to convince yourself you deserve to be there anyway.

She glanced at the main stage, where the first speaker was already halfway through a talk on KPIs and fiscal-year alignment. Camryn tried to follow, but the words washed over her like hotel lobby music, both audible and forgettable. She caught a few buzzwords she recognized from budget meetings: efficiency, synergy, and optimization, but they slid through her like vapor.

She nodded along out of habit, but inside she was somewhere else entirely. She scanned the room. Polished leaders nodded in agreement. Fingers flew across tablets. She felt like an actor trapped in the wrong scene. Her imposter syndrome was loud. Her instincts told her to shrink.

Then came the next speaker.

A Black woman. Poised, grounded, radiating something Camryn couldn't name at first. She wasn't loud. She wasn't flashy. But she carried herself as if she belonged to herself. Bold red lipstick. Chunky earrings. A navy suit that made a statement without saying a word. But it wasn't the outfit that held the room.

It was the way she stood. The way she breathed. The way her eyes met people, not just the front row, but even the ones like Camryn, posted up by the exit.

Ultimately, it was the way she started.

"I wasn't always confident," she said, smiling with her whole face. "I built her."

Camryn felt her breath catch.

The woman didn't open with her credentials. She opened with her truth. She spoke about her self-care routines and about talking to herself in the mirror until her voice no longer shook. About the early days when she said "yes" to everything out of fear, and the later days when she learned to say "no" without guilt. About walking into boardrooms where no one expected her to lead, and leading anyway. Not without trembling, but with intention. She shared how she learned to pause before she spoke, not because she was unsure, but because she understood the value of silence.

"Confidence," she said, "isn't magic. It's a series of small, sacred decisions you make before you feel ready. Over and over again."

Camryn's throat tightened. She didn't know why she suddenly felt like crying. Maybe because someone had finally said the quiet part out loud, that confidence isn't inherited or intuitive. It's curated. And women like her had been curating it in silence for years.

That night, back at the hotel, Camryn stood in front of the full-length mirror bolted to the closet door. The fluorescent lighting wasn't kind, but she didn't flinch. She stared at her reflection, the same one she'd avoided before interviews, big meetings, even dates. Her blazer was still on. Her heels were kicked off near the bed. Her edges had frizzed a little from the day's stress sweat.

She looked… unfinished. Human. Like a work in motion.

She didn't ask, "Am I enough?"

She whispered, "You already are."

Then, without planning to, she pulled out a notebook she had packed in her carry-on, the worn one she always packed but rarely used. She flipped past old grocery lists and sermon notes to a blank page and wrote three truths:

1. I don't need to wait until I feel confident to move.

2. My voice is worth hearing, even when it trembles.

3. I'm not seeking a crown. I'm remembering that I already wear one.

The pen dug into the page like a promise. Not a hope. A decision.

The next morning, Camryn woke up with a quiet resolve. She decided that, from that day forward, she would do small things differently.

At work, she stopped leading with disclaimers.

"This might be silly, but…" became "Here's what I'm proposing."

She didn't shrink before she spoke. She didn't wait to be invited.

She started wearing clothes that made her feel like herself, not what the boardroom expected, but what her body loved. Soft fabrics, bold colors, pieces that whispered: This is me.

She scheduled a recurring Monday morning calendar block titled "Return to Self." No meetings. No email. Just her. A mirror. A playlist. And the quiet ritual of reminding herself: *You belong here. You're not an exception. You're the example.*

She reached out to a woman she admired, a VP who once pulled her aside after a panel and said, "Don't ever let them tame your magic." Camryn asked for a virtual coffee chat, heart pounding as she hit send. To her surprise, the VP replied within the hour: "Absolutely. Let's talk."

They didn't just talk about career moves. They spoke of confidence, yes, but also about burnout. About the pressure to outperform. About the fear of being labeled angry when you're just being honest. About learning to rest without guilt.

They talked about imposter syndrome. About the quiet ache of wanting to rest but not knowing how. The kind of rest that comes only when you stop trying to prove your worth in every room you enter.

Camryn realized something after that meeting: confidence wasn't about being the loudest in the room. It wasn't about polished speeches or perfect posture.

It was about being the most rooted in your *why*.

A month later, she attended another leadership conference. This time, she sat closer to the front. Not in the spotlight, but not in the shadows either. She asked a question during the Q&A, not rehearsed, not perfect, but hers.

During the networking break, a younger woman approached her: wide eyes, nervous smile, hesitant steps, soft voice.

"Hi... I just wanted to say... I saw you speak during the Q&A. You were so clear and grounded. I hope I can carry myself like that one day."

Camryn blinked.

Her? Clear? Grounded?

She smiled. Not out of modesty. Out of recognition. Because she saw herself in the woman's eyes, the uncertainty, the hunger, the becoming.

"You already do," Camryn said gently. "You just haven't realized it yet. But you will."

That night, back in her hotel room, she stood in front of the mirror again. Same lighting. Same body. Same eyes.

But this time, she didn't brace herself.

She smiled. Not to practice. Not to impress. Just... to honor the woman who had built herself, brick by brick, affirmation by affirmation.

And when she whispered, "You belong here," she believed it.

Because the crown wasn't something she found in a room.

It was something she had forged in silence.

And finally, she wore it without apology.

AUTHOR'S REFLECTION: I STOPPED WAITING TO FEEL READY. I STARTED MOVING LIKE I BELONGED.

Confidence didn't come to me like a lightning bolt. It wasn't something I "found." It was something I *curated*.

Piece by piece.

Decision by decision.

Boundary by boundary.

I realized early on that confidence wasn't about being the loudest in the room.

It was about being the most rooted in your *why*.

And my why was bigger than me.

So I started building my confidence the way a curator builds a gallery, intentionally.

I gathered what empowered me.

I released what diminished me.

And slowly, I created a life I could walk through without shrinking.

I Rewrote the Script in My Mind

The voices in my head used to sound like:

- Don't mess this up.
- They're going to find out you don't belong.
- You're only here because of luck or pity.

So I got louder.

With truth.

I started feeding myself new thoughts, on purpose.

From books.

From sermons.

From podcasts.

From the Word.

From women who had walked the road ahead of me.

And when I couldn't find the words I needed, I wrote them myself.

I stood in the mirror and practiced believing

I didn't wait to feel confident to act confident.

I practiced it like a routine to grow my muscles.

I stood in front of the mirror and said things like:

"You are powerful. Even when you're tired."

"You are worthy of this role. You're not an exception, you're an example."

"If God placed you here, then there is purpose here."

Sometimes my voice shook.

Sometimes I cried.

Sometimes I rolled my eyes at myself.

But I showed up anyway.

And over time, the mirror stopped reflecting doubt. It started reflecting the *truth*.

I Sought Mentors, Not Just for Answers, but for Anchoring

I sought out women who didn't just look polished; they looked **free**.

Women who walked in a room and didn't shrink. Women who made space, not just took up space.

Some were formal mentors. Others were just quiet guides who spoke life over me in passing moments.

But every one of them reminded me:

"You don't have to know everything to lead. You just have to be honest, prepared, and present."

I Aligned My Life With My Mission

The biggest confidence booster of all?

Living in alignment.

Once I got clear on my personal mission, who I serve, why I lead, what I will and won't compromise, my decisions got easier.

I stopped saying yes to what looked good on paper but felt hollow in my spirit. I stopped working for validation and started working from vision.

Confidence isn't loud.

It's *quiet certainty*.

It's peace that you're where you're supposed to be.

Confidence Is Not a Personality Trait; It's a Practice.

You don't wait for it. You *build* it.

Every time you speak up when it's hard.

Every time you say no when it's scary.

Every time you show up in your fullness, knowing someone might flinch, but you're going to flourish anyway,

You are curating confidence.

And it shows.

REFLECTION PROMPT FOR THE READER:

What's a belief about yourself that you're ready to rewrite?

_____

_____

_____

_____

Who are the confident women you admire, and what can you borrow from their example?

_____

_____

_____

_____

What does living in alignment look like for you right now?

_____

_____

_____

_____

CHAPTER 5
CAMRYN'S STORY: THE MIC AND THE MOMENT

The microphone felt heavier than Camryn expected, like it had soaked up every speech that had come before hers, every trembling confession and hollow cliché, and now demanded to know which one she planned to add to its history. It was ice-cold, a thin cylinder of metal that bit into her palms and reminded her of the subzero winters she grew up in back home.

Backstage smelled of sawdust and fresh paint, and the fine coating of wetness covered the hardwoods from stage fog that hadn't evaporated yet. Footsteps thudded on the scuffed floorboards. Someone yanked a curtain rope, releasing a puff of dust that danced in the bright yellow stage light. Camryn's notecards, now damp from being clutched in her sweaty palms, fluttered like anxious wings between her fingertips.

The emcee's voice boomed across the auditorium, confident and loud as he said:

"Please welcome today's keynote speaker… Camryn J. Morgan!"

Applause erupted, polite, dutiful, filling the air like confetti she couldn't quite see. Camryn's heart thudded up into her throat, then settled somewhere behind her eyes, pulsing at her temples. She took one last breath, deep enough to reach the shy child who used to hide behind her bedroom door, making up fantastical stories she never told anyone. Then she stepped into the light.

The stage lights blazed white-hot, blurring the first row. She squinted, spotted empty mugs on the moderator's table, and half-eaten pastries abandoned on napkins. A soft murmur rippled as people adjusted in their chairs, professionals in pressed shirts and polished loafers, mostly white, mostly comfortable in spaces like this. Some looked interested; some scrolled discreetly on their phones; a few gave the tight, close-lipped grin reserved for obligatory curiosity. No one looked like her. Her brown skin was glowing under lights that began to feel hot, like rays of sunlight, causing Camryn to perspire, and the edges of her hairline, smoothed flat this morning with castor oil and prayer, began to coil up under the oppressive stage lights.

The voice in her head taunted, as loud as a PA system: *They don't want your real story. Keep it light, keep it safe. Give them what they expect: statistics and sanitized metaphors. Not roaches, not food stamps, not cabinets that stayed empty until payday.*

Camryn glanced down at her top note card. The first sentence stared back, black ink thick and blunt:

"I come from leaky ceilings and eviction notices, not corner offices."

Her hands trembled, and her palms were so moist you could wring them out like a dishcloth. A tidal wave of nerves flowed through her body like a tremor that started in her fingertips and rippled up her forearms. Her tongue felt like cotton, mouth dry from a paralyzing fear so familiar she could almost call it by name. But this time, this first real time, she didn't back down.

She stood in the center of the stage with heels planted in the floor like punctuation. The spotlight felt like noon in July, scorching her scalp. She cleared her throat; the mic captured every rasp of nerves.

"Good afternoon." Her voice cracked on "good," and wobbled on "afternoon." A ripple of shifting bodies, a single cough, then silence. She braced herself and spoke the sentence anyway.

"I come from leaky ceilings and eviction notices, not corner offices."

The words dropped like a stone into water, sending rings of startled quiet through the room. She felt the audience lean, felt the hush thicken. Somewhere near the back, a laptop snapped shut, as if someone decided spreadsheets could wait.

She told them about mouse traps under every kitchen cabinet, about the shame of late notice envelopes stamped **FINAL WARNING** in red ink. About being a single, twenty-five-year-old college dropout, handing over food stamp cards at the register while staring straight ahead so she couldn't see pity in the cashier's eyes. About the first job where she learned to code-switch so hard her voice turned into a rehearsed accent she barely recognized.

She spoke of panic attacks in bathroom stalls, how the scent of cheap lavender air freshener still made her palms sweat, because it reminded her of trying to slow her breathing. At the same time, colleagues on the other side gossiped about how her hair changed every few weeks, as if her protective styles were fashion statements rather than armor.

She held nothing back: 4:00 a.m. bus rides, bargain blazers that shone too bright under fluorescent lights, the queasy thrill of making it to a meeting only to feel like an intruder in a glass-walled conference room. She talked about reading leadership books after double shifts, highlighting passages that felt aspirational and impossible all at once. And finally, she told them about choosing herself anyway, even when it was hard, especially when it was hard.

Somewhere between the story of borrowing gas money for an interview and the confession that she once practiced saying "strategy" in a deeper register to make it sound more authoritative, the room went still. No rustling, no side talk, just listening so intently she could hear the whir of the A/C above the stage.

Halfway through, Camryn lifted her gaze and locked eyes with a woman in the second row, in a sky-grey suit, tight curls, eyes glossy with unshed tears. A single tear finally slid down the woman's cheek, and her hand pressed flat against her heart. In that tiny shared second, Camryn felt something break open, not painful, but like a seed casing splitting so the green shoot could grow.

She finished without rushing, without editing, without shrinking. When the last line dropped, *"The goal isn't to be fearless. It's to move while still afraid and let fear watch you win."* The silence held, thick and heavy, for exactly three heartbeats. Then it shattered into applause.

Real applause. Not polite. Not obligatory. Applause that thumped in her chest, applause that felt like hands catching her mid-freefall. She exhaled a breath she didn't know she was holding, felt it rush out, warm and alive.

Afterward, a line formed, people she didn't know, people who suddenly seemed to know her. A CEO with perfectly square spectacles grasped Camryn's shoulder and said, voice unsteady, "Thank you for reminding me why I started." A young intern with chipped nail polish hugged her so tight it hurt and whispered, "You said the thing I thought I had to swallow forever. Thank you for saying the quiet part out loud." Others touched her arm, pressed notes into her palm, phone numbers, invitations, and gratitude scribbled on program flyers. The air smelled of perfume and possibility, of nerves turned electric waves of confidence throughout her body.

Camryn smiled, the kind of smile that comes from a deep exhale, the kind that says, *I almost didn't say it. But I'm so glad I did.*

Hours later, the applause still echoed in her bloodstream as she slipped her keycard into the hotel room door. The hallway hush felt exaggerated after the roar of validation. Inside, the room lights blinked on, soft, yellow, and forgiving. She kicked off her shoes, feeling the plush carpet under her swollen feet. The mirror on the wardrobe reflected a version of her she hadn't met before, eyes rimmed with leftover mascara, cheeks glowing with exhaustion and something brighter, something that wasn't painted on. Something akin to confidence and triumph.

The adrenaline had faded, but the fear had not. It hovered near her shoulders like a shadow companion. But something else was vying for that coveted spot taken up by fear for far too long: a quiet, unshakeable knowing.

She tugged her journal from her tote, the cover bent, pages feathered with sticky notes. She sat cross-legged on the duvet, flipped to a clean page, and wrote:

My voice shook. But it still carried.

My hands trembled. But they held the mic.

Fear rode shotgun. But it never touched the steering wheel.

She paused, listening to the hush around her, the hum of the mini fridge, the distant elevator ding. She could almost hear the younger version of herself cheering, banging on bedroom walls, crying, and yelling *FINALLY*.

She kept writing.

I won't conquer fear. We'll coexist. I'll give it a seat, but never the stage.

Tonight proved what I already suspected: Truth tastes like freedom, and everyone's hungry.

Camryn closed the journal, pressed her palm to the cover, as if sealing an envelope full of sacred news. Then she approached the mirror one more time, bare-faced and dog-tired. She lifted the stiff-bristle brush, doubling as a makeshift microphone.

She held the microphone brush up to her face, just below her lips, and whispered, for herself alone, "Thank you for trusting me."

She knew she would stand in front of a crowd again, mic trembling slightly, heart sprinting. She knew fear would show up too, punctual as ever. But she also knew, deep down in her bones, deeper than fear, that her story had room to breathe on any stage she chose to stand on.

And next time, the mic would not feel heavy.

It would feel like home.

AUTHOR'S REFLECTION: I BROUGHT MY DOUBTS WITH ME AND DID IT ANYWAY

Fear used to run the show.

It was dressed up like overthinking.

It pretended to be humility. It whispered:

- What if you're wrong?
- What if you fail publicly?

- What if they finally realize you're not as good as they think?

I used to think I needed to get rid of fear before I could lead. But one day, I decided:

Fear doesn't get to drive, but it can ride in the passenger seat.

That was the beginning of my freedom.

I Stopped Trying to "Conquer" Fear, and Started Listening to It

I learned that fear isn't always the enemy.

Sometimes, it's a signal.

A protector.

A wounded inner voice that just wants to keep you safe.

So instead of pushing fear away, I started saying:

"I see you. But I'm not following you anymore."

I gave my fear a front row seat, right next to shame, guilt, and grief. And then I got on the mic anyway.

My Voice Shook, But I Still Spoke

I can't count how many times I spoke up in rooms where my voice trembled.

Or how many keynotes I gave with my palms sweaty and my heart pounding.

But here's what I've learned:

A shaky voice is still a voice.

And your truth doesn't need to be perfectly delivered to land exactly where it's needed.

Every time I spoke while afraid, I expanded.

Every time I showed up afraid, I showed others what's possible.

That's how legacy works.

Courage Isn't the Absence of Fear; It's Faith in Action

You want to know what else was in the room with my fear?

Purpose.

Anointing.

Generations of women who didn't have the chance to sit in the spaces I occupy.

My fear isn't bigger than *that*.

You Don't Need to Be Ready. You Need to Be Willing.

If you're waiting to feel 100% confident before you act, you'll be stuck forever. The secret is: none of us feels ready. We just show up anyway.

Leadership isn't about waiting until you've healed everything. It's about moving while the healing is happening.

And when you do that?

You don't just silence your fear. You humble it.

REFLECTION PROMPT FOR THE READER:

What is fear currently keeping you from doing?

_____

_____

_____

_____

What would it look like to invite fear along, but not let it lead?

_____

_____

_____

_____

What truth do you need to speak, even if your voice shakes?

_____

_____

_____

_____

CHAPTER 6
CAMRYN'S STORY: NO SEAT AT THE TABLE

Camryn knew she was overdressed.

She could feel it in the way the receptionist's eyes flicked down to her heels, then back up, deliberately polite but holding that quiet "you tried too hard" judgment she'd come to recognize over the years.

She smoothed the lapel of her navy blue blazer, freshly steamed and smelling faintly of starch and lavender from the little spray bottle she carried in her purse, and reminded herself why she was here.

Her first strategy meeting as Director.

She repeated the words in her head like an incantation, as if saying them enough times would make them belong to her. Director. Director. Director.

Her palms were damp against the leather strap of her tote bag, where she'd stuffed three pens, two highlighters, an entire notebook, and a bottle of water she probably wouldn't drink.

The conference room door stood slightly ajar, and she could already hear them inside: the muffled rumble of low laughter, chairs scraping hardwood, the thud of ceramic mugs on the table.

She hesitated, heart hammering, every nerve ending on alert.

The Room

When she finally stepped in, the air felt different; cooler, filtered, with the faint antiseptic scent of money and power. The hum of the vent overhead mingled with the soft whir of a projector fan.

Twelve leather chairs circled an oval mahogany table polished so cleanly she could see the reflection of the recessed ceiling lights ripple across its surface.

People were already seated, leaning back like they owned the air itself, voices casual but firm, confident in their belonging—crisp white shirts, slim watches, silk ties, understated jewelry; wealth without trying too hard.

She scanned the room instinctively, counting: ten men, two women. Eleven white faces, one Black. Hers.

No one looked up right away.

Her chest tightened. She forced herself to inhale, square her shoulders, and slide into a chair halfway down the table; not too close to the head, not too far at the end—neutral ground.

But the seat felt colder than the air-conditioned room, more frigid than the looks that eventually found her, one by one, taking her in like an unfamiliar variable in an otherwise predictable equation.

"Camryn, right?" one of them asked, glancing at his watch before returning to his laptop.

She nodded, managing a polite smile.

The Weight of Silence

The meeting began. PowerPoint slides clicked. Acronyms flew through the air like confetti she couldn't catch fast enough; ROI, HEDIS, EBITDA, STAR ratings, MLR.

Her pen moved furiously across the page, but the words blurred. Her brain kept looping the same thought:

Don't look confused. Don't look green. Don't give them a reason to think you don't belong here.

She tried to match their rhythm, the cadence of their clipped voices, the confidence in their pauses. But the jargon stacked faster than she could translate, and the more they spoke, the more the walls seemed to close in.

Then, halfway through, the tension shifted.

They started discussing **budget cuts**; quietly at first, then louder, as if volume itself could make the decision righteous.

"We need to trim costs on community programs," one executive said, his tone flat, surgical. "The outreach numbers just aren't justifying the spend."

Camryn's stomach knotted. She knew those programs. She'd built relationships with the families they served, hugged grandmothers in church basements, sat at folding tables handing out groceries in neighborhoods where grocery stores had vanished.

Cutting funding wasn't just a line item. It was oxygen.

Her pen stilled.

The Decision

Camryn felt it rising, the words in her chest, the quiet rebellion of her entire being saying: *Say something.*

But her throat tightened.

She glanced around the table. No one else seemed bothered. One person nodded. Another scrolled on his phone. The leader at the head of the table rubbed his temple as if this was already settled.

She heard her mother's voice then, uninvited but grounding:

"Baby, closed mouths don't get fed. You weren't raised to watch and say nothing."

Her heart thudded so loudly she thought someone would notice. She flexed her fingers under the table, nails digging into her palm, grounding herself.

And then, before she could talk herself out of it, she cleared her throat.

"Excuse me," she said.

Twelve heads turned.

Her voice almost failed, a rasp stuck at the edge of fear. But she pressed on.

"I… I think we need to reconsider cutting that funding," she said, slower now, each word pulled from someplace deeper than her résumé. "That 'spend' you're talking about; those are people. Those programs connect families to food, medications, and transportation. Cutting them doesn't just impact metrics. It changes lives."

The silence stretched.

Someone clicked a pen. A coffee mug hit the table with a dull thud.

Finally, the man two seats down leaned back and smirked slightly, his tone clipped.

"That's a great point, Camryn," he said, polite enough to sound supportive but patronizing enough to slice. "But we're talking sustainability here. Emotional appeals can't drive fiscal strategy."

The words landed sharp, intentional. The subtext was louder than his tone: *Know your place.*

Her cheeks burned. Her ears buzzed. She wanted to shrink. But something in her refused.

She sat taller.

"With respect," she said, steady now, "it's not an emotional appeal. It's evidence. The data show that when we invest upstream in food security, transportation, and access, we reduce ER visits, lower readmissions, and improve quality metrics. That *is* a fiscal strategy. People are strategy."

She held his gaze this time.

The Shift

The room stilled again, but differently now.

Someone at the far end leaned forward. "She's right," he said slowly, almost begrudgingly. "There *is* a correlation between outreach investment and STAR ratings."

Others murmured. Someone pulled up a spreadsheet.

And just like that, the conversation shifted.

Not entirely, they didn't suddenly become champions of equity overnight, but the energy tilted. The possibility cracked open.

Camryn breathed in quietly, shoulders easing just enough to release the knot between her blades.

For the first time all morning, she felt her feet planted beneath the table.

After the Meeting

When it ended, people shuffled out quickly, murmuring to each other about follow-up tasks. No one patted her back. No one praised her courage.

She stayed seated until the room was almost empty, her pulse finally slowing, hands flat on the polished wood.

Her reflection in the table stared back at her, a little sweaty, a little shaky, but still there.

She thought about what had almost happened. How close she'd come to swallowing her words, to nodding along, to disappearing into silence because it felt safer.

But she didn't.

She'd spoken.

And though her voice had wavered, it had landed.

The Knowing

Back at her desk later, Camryn pulled out her journal, flipping to a fresh page. Her handwriting shook slightly, but the ink held steady:

Today, I learned the room doesn't hand you power.

The table doesn't save you a seat.

You carve it. You claim it. You build it when it doesn't exist.

She underlined it twice, the pen digging grooves into the page.

Because that was the truth, no leadership book had prepared her for:

Power isn't given. It's taken, then stewarded.

And maybe, she thought, that was the point of being here at all.

Not to blend in.

To build differently.

AUTHOR'S REFLECTION: WHAT HAPPENS WHEN YOU STOP SHRINKING AND START SHOWING UP

It started slowly.

A message here.

An email there.

A quiet *"Hey sis, I see you."*

Then came the invitations:

- Could you speak at this event?
- Would you be our keynote?
- Can we feature you in this campaign?

I said yes.

Even when I was nervous.

Even when I didn't think I was "ready."

Even when I didn't feel like I looked like the women who usually stood at that mic.

And suddenly, I became the poster girl for *bridging out of poverty*, for *resilience*, for *becoming*.

It felt surreal.

It felt divine.

And sometimes, it felt heavy.

Because with visibility comes responsibility.

The Shift Wasn't That I Became "More Qualified", It's That I Became *More Visible*

I was already capable before the invitations came. I just wasn't always seen.

But the moment I started showing up fully, braids, brilliance, Black art and all, the world caught up.

The shift was never in my qualifications. It was in my alignment.

People don't respond to perfection.

They respond to **presence.**

To truth.

To the kind of leadership that feels like home.

Keynotes, Commercials, and the Cost of the Spotlight

I've stood on stages for the NAACP.

I've addressed national organizations, such as the NADSP.

I've been the face of campaigns and commercials that highlight triumph and transformation.

Each time, I carried my story like a sacred offering.

Not polished. Not rehearsed to perfection. But *real.*

And every time someone came up to me afterward and said, *"Thank you. I needed to hear that,"* I was reminded:

This isn't performance. It's purpose.

But I won't lie, visibility has a cost.

The more people saw me, the more I had to protect my peace.

The more I gave to the world, the more I had to reclaim time for myself.

The more I stood in the light, the more intentional I had to be about not burning out in it.

When You Show Up Fully, You Give Others Permission to Do the Same

Every time I showed up scared but grounded,

Every time I told the truth instead of the script,

Every time I made space for joy and not just performance,

Other women stepped forward, too.

That's what the invitations really meant. Not just *"we see you,"* but *"we need more of what you carry."*

REFLECTION PROMPT FOR THE READER:

What would you do if you stopped waiting to be ready?

Where might you already be invited, but fear is muting your response?

How can your story create space for someone else's voice?

PART

Two

THE UNLEARNING

CHAPTER 7
CAMRYN'S STORY: THE WEIGHT OF THE BLAZER

It wasn't just a blazer.

It was armor.

Navy blue, tailored just enough to give the illusion of confidence. Shoulder pads slightly too wide, lapels stiff with starch. Camryn had found it on clearance at a department store the year she got her first "real" job after returning to college, fresh out of grad school. She wore it to every interview, every panel, every presentation that felt too big for her.

It made her look the part; she told herself.

It made her invisible in all the right ways.

Today, she stood in her bedroom, holding the blazer by the hanger, staring at it as if it had betrayed her. Another DEI panel. Another room full of polite nods and invisible boundaries. Another hour of choosing her words carefully enough to educate, but not offend.

She laid the blazer on the bed and exhaled.

It still carried the scent of old perfume and nervous sweat. It smelled like assimilation. Like anxiety in fabric form. Like the version of her that apologized for taking up space.

She sat on the edge of the bed, blazer beside her like a question:

Are you going to disappear again today?

Her mind drifted to past moments that had shaped her silence.

The time she was called "aggressive" for disagreeing in a meeting, after a male colleague had interrupted the dialogue three times, and no one blinked.

The time a supervisor pulled her aside after a passionate presentation and said, "You should smile more. You have such a powerful presence when you're softer."

The time she got the invite to a "diversity dialogue" but not the budget meeting.

The time she chose silence because she was tired of being "the only."

Camryn stood and walked to her closet. She stared at the rows of clothes that told the story of a woman who had mastered the art of fitting in.

Muted tones. Simple lines. Neutral everything.

Professional.

Palatable.

Safe.

Her hands hovered, then moved past the blazer. She reached for something else, a deep green wrap dress that hugged her curves and reminded her of her aunties down South. She pulled it from the hanger and smiled.

Next, her jewelry drawer. She found her favorite gold hoops, the ones her aunt once called "armor of joy." She put them on. They felt like rebellion. They felt like freedom.

She styled her hair in a high puff, no gel, no apology. Just her. Coiled, confident, whole.

An hour later, she stepped into the conference space and was greeted with the usual buzz. Name tags. Notepads. Bottled water. A moderator with practiced charm.

Camryn sat on the far end of the panel table. Her dress swished softly as she crossed her legs. She smiled, not the tight, polite one she'd worn for years, but the grounded kind. The kind that says, *I didn't come here to shrink.*

The panel began.

Halfway through, someone in the audience asked a question that changed the air.

"What does it really feel like to lead as a woman of color in systems that weren't built for you?"

Camryn didn't rush. She let the silence stretch just long enough to make the room lean in.

Then she spoke.

"It feels like walking a tightrope with no net," she said. "It feels like having to explain your value over and over again in rooms that invited you in for perspective but not power. It feels like watching people flinch at your clarity and then call it 'intimidating.' It feels like carrying your ancestors and your community on your back while pretending it's not heavy."

The room was still.

"I've worn the blazer," she added. "I've played the part. But I'm done dressing myself in someone else's comfort. I came here as all of me."

A beat.

Then applause.

Not everyone clapped. But Camryn didn't need them to.

After the panel, a young woman with tight curls and wide eyes approached her, hesitantly.

"I just wanted to say… You helped me feel seen today. I almost didn't come because I've been so tired of being the 'diversity' in the room. But seeing you show up like that? It made me feel like maybe I can, too."

Camryn touched the gold hoop on her left ear and smiled.

"You can. And not just here. Everywhere."

That night, back at home, she opened her closet and moved the navy blazer to the back.

She didn't throw it away.

She just... outgrew it.

AUTHOR'S REFLECTION: HOW I STAYED WHOLE IN A WORLD THAT WANTED ME SMALL

There's a difference between being in the room and being *seen* in the room.

I've been in rooms with credentials, degrees, a strong résumé, and lived experience that could shift systems, and still felt invisible.

Why?

Because some spaces are designed to make you question your enoughness.

They reward quiet.

They reward conformity.

They reward proximity to whiteness, maleness, thinness, softness, whatever "safe" looks like in that system.

And if you don't match it?

You start to feel like a problem that needs fixing.

My leadership isn't just about me.

It's for every young Black girl wondering if she's too loud, too dark, too poor, too curvy, or too "different" to make it.

It's for every woman who feels like she's leading at a deficit because she wasn't born into a boardroom.

I didn't have a hand to hold on my way up. So I became one.

It's for my children, **both of them**, who reflect different parts of my why.

For **Shaun**, my firstborn, my original catalyst.

A quiet warrior with a global spirit and music in his soul.

He's stood beside me in boardrooms and airports, on mission trips and hotel lobbies. He's served humbly, created music that moves people from the inside out, and built a life grounded in integrity, talent, and quiet strength.

Shaun doesn't speak often, but when he does, it matters.

He's the reminder that leadership isn't always loud.

That brilliance doesn't always need applause.

And that your impact can fill a room without ever raising your voice.

And for **Brandon**, my son born with Down syndrome when I was just 20, who taught me to slow down, love harder, and advocate relentlessly.

He gave me the fire. He made the injustice personal and ensured my leadership was purposeful.

These two boys are my roots and my wings.

They are why I don't back down.

Why I speak up.

Why I show up.

This blueprint is for women, but it's also for them.

Because I want them to see a mother who didn't just survive.

I want them to know that love can be fierce, soft, strategic, and sacred, all at once.

Assimilation is not the same as belonging

I learned early on how to adjust.

How to keep my voice just below "too direct."

How to straighten my hair and soften my brilliance.

How to be exceptional, but not threatening.

That's the game.

You learn how to survive in systems that were never built with you in mind.

But surviving isn't the same as *leading*. It's not the same as *living*.

Eventually, I had to choose:

Am I going to keep shape shifting to make others comfortable, or am I going to take up the space I was created for?

Poverty Taught Me How to Grind. Leadership Taught Me How to Heal.

Growing up with lack taught me how to over function.

How to outwork, overprove, and never rest.

How to believe that value is earned through exhaustion.

But leadership taught me something else:

Rest is a form of resistance.

Presence is power.

I don't have to bleed for my seat.

The systems won't always change overnight.

But *I* could change the way I moved through them.

And that changed everything.

You Are Not "Too Much." The Room Might Just Be Too Small.

If you've ever been labeled difficult, aggressive, intimidating, emotional, or *not a team player* for simply being *clear*, you are not the problem.

You are the recalibration.

Let that sink in.

REFLECTION PROMPT FOR THE READER:

Where have you been asked to shrink or shift in order to succeed?

_____

_____

_____

_____

Which systems or stereotypes have you internalized, and are you ready to release them?

_____

_____

_____

_____

What would it look like to take up your full, unedited space?

_____

_____

_____

_____

CHAPTER 8
CAMRYN'S STORY: THE BENCH UNDER THE OAK TREE

Camryn hadn't meant to stop walking.

She was just out for some air, trying to shake the weight of another meeting where she'd been the only one to mention equity, and the only one ignored. Her heels clicked softly against the cracked sidewalk as she wandered away from the office, letting instinct, not destination, guide her feet. She walked past the coffee shop with its clinking mugs, past the bookstore where bell chimes greeted customers, and into a side street she'd never taken before.

That's when she saw it.

The tree.

An oak, massive, ancient, magnificent. Its bark was rough, with deep grooves like carved scripture, as if it carried the stories of everyone who had ever leaned against it. Its trunk stretched wide enough to hold generations of secrets, and its limbs reached toward the sky as if offering prayers. Beneath it sat a wooden bench; weathered but sturdy, edges worn smooth by time and touch. It looked as though it had been waiting for her.

Camryn hesitated, scanning the quiet park around her. The city noises dulled here. The hum of traffic melted into birdsong, and somewhere nearby, the soft rush of wind danced through leaves. She stepped off the path and made her way toward the bench, each step sinking slightly into the earth beneath her heels.

When she sat, the bench gave a soft, tired creak, as if exhaling under her weight. Camryn inhaled slowly, observing the dampness of early spring in the air; the scent of rain-soaked earth, magnolia blossoms, and distant cut grass. She didn't reach for her phone. She didn't open her planner. She just sat and breathed, like her body knew what her mind hadn't yet realized:

She needed this pause.

And then… she felt them.

Not seen. Not heard. But known.

The women.

The ones who came before her. The ones who carved the path she was walking, brick by brick, prayer by prayer. She felt them the way you feel warmth on your skin before the sun rises. The presence was soft, but undeniable.

She thought of her mother, who raised her while raising herself. A woman who made miracles out of food stamps and faith, who stretched dollars and hope in equal measure. Her voice still lived inside Camryn's bones, gentle but firm: "Baby, keep your head high, even when your pockets are empty."

She thought of her grandmothers; women who survived entire decades without titles or applause, whose hands told stories that history books never would. Women who bore heavy loads with quiet grace, carrying whole families on their backs without permission to break.

She thought of her aunties down South; the ones who led from kitchen tables and salon chairs, who healed communities with their laughter, wisdom, and fried chicken wrapped in foil; women who didn't have degrees but carried doctorates in survival.

And she felt them, here, beneath this oak tree.

It was as though they sat beside her, folding laundry in her spirit, nodding the way Black women do when they don't need words to say, *We see you. We've been you. Keep going.*

Camryn closed her eyes and let the warmth of it wash over her.

The wind stirred again, lifting loose strands of her hair and carrying the scent of earth and sunlight. Camryn reached into her bag, pulled out her journal, and pressed pen to paper.

"I don't lead alone," she wrote. *"I walk in their prayers. I speak what they were never allowed to say. I carry more than strategy, I carry names."*

She stopped, letting the weight of those words settle, and then underlined them twice.

For a moment, it felt like the oak itself leaned in. Like the whispers of those who came before her brushed against her skin:

"We're proud of you. Don't stop now."

Her throat tightened, but she didn't cry. Not here. Not under this tree, where strength and softness met.

She sat in that silence a little longer, feeling the hum of belonging rise in her chest. When she finally stood, it wasn't because the moment had passed; it was because it had rooted itself inside her.

Camryn walked away from that bench knowing something had shifted.

She didn't just have a platform.

She had a calling.

Not to be seen.

To be useful.

To build something that would outlive her.

To speak for the women still silenced.

And to leave the door wide open behind her.

AUTHOR'S REFLECTION: I LEAD BECAUSE SOMEONE HAS TO, AND IF NOT ME, THEN WHO?

I didn't wake up one day and decide to be an advocate. I *became* one in the fire.

It happened every time I was overlooked.

Every time my child was underestimated.

Every time I sat at a table and realized I was the only one asking, *"But what about the ones who aren't in this room?"*

My leadership is *loud* on purpose.

It is *unapologetic* on purpose.

Because silence never saved me.

And it won't save the women, the children, the communities I'm here to serve.

When I have challenging moments as a leader, I think of my sons.

My youngest was born with a diagnosis and a destiny. A boy who made injustice personal, whose existence taught me that advocacy wasn't a career, it was survival. Loving him cracked me wide open, teaching me understanding and compassion deeper than anything I can gain from textbooks and fight more fiercely than any I've had in a boardroom.

My eldest, my quiet compass. The dreamer. The artist. The one who leads with spirit, not spectacle. From him, I have learned that real leadership doesn't always shout; sometimes it lives, steady and grounded, even when the world feels loud.

Brandon Made It Personal

When Brandon was born with Down syndrome, I was just 20 years old.

Young.

Black.

Single.

Poor.

Unprepared

YET - determined.

I wasn't just fighting for a better life anymore.

I was fighting for someone who would one day need the world to see his full humanity.

He lit the fire.

He taught me that **equity isn't optional.**

That access isn't enough.

That every system: healthcare, education, and employment, has cracks wide enough to lose the most vulnerable in.

Brandon taught me how to lead not from theory, but from truth.

From the doctor's office.

From the IEP meeting.

From the advocacy calls no one sees behind the scenes.

I am the mother, the nurse, the speaker, the woman I *needed* to navigate the systems that were never designed for us.

Shaun Taught Me What Quiet Leadership Looks Like

Shaun, my firstborn, my compass, He leads differently.

He doesn't raise his voice often, but he *moves* people.

He's served in Ghana with me on a mission trip.

He has volunteered in the community for back-to-school giveaways, Meals on Wheels, Rescue Mission soup kitchen, and so much more.

He's produced music for artists and labels that reach hearts and ears around the globe. He stands tall in rooms where he doesn't need to dominate; his presence speaks for itself.

He reminded me that leadership isn't always loud.

Sometimes it's steady.

Spiritual.

Creative.

Grounded.

Shaun carries the legacy of those who lead by example. The kind of men the world needs more of.

And I carry him in every space I enter, too.

Advocacy Is Bigger Than Policy, It's Personal

Advocacy isn't just something I do. It's something I *am*.

It's in the way I challenge systems with grace and clarity.

It's in the way I lift others with strategy, not saviorism.

It's in the way I call out injustice, even when it's uncomfortable, even when I'm the only one saying it.

And it's ancestral.

I carry the strength of women who never had a voice.

I carry the hope of sons who deserve a better future.

I carry the wisdom of communities that survive in systems not built for them.

So I lead.

Loudly, clearly, humbly, and purposefully. Because someone has to.

And if not me, then who?

REFLECTION PROMPT FOR THE READER:

What injustice or inequity feels personal to you?

_____

_____

_____

_____

Where do you feel called to lead, not just for yourself, but for others?

_____

_____

_____

_____

What would advocacy look like in your current role or daily life?

_____

_____

_____

_____

CHAPTER 9
CAMRYN'S STORY: THE DOOR WITHOUT A HANDLE

From time to time, Camryn would have vivid dreams that would lead her to an epiphany and renewed strength to keep moving forward. One dream took her down a long hallway. The hallway stretched endlessly, sterile and soundless. It was lined with crisp white walls and polished tile that reflected the fluorescent lights above like a mirror to her uncertainty. The soft hum overhead buzzed in rhythm with her nerves. Her heels clicked with intention, but her heart stuttered with every step.

Camryn walked slowly, deliberately, as though the corridor might vanish if she moved too fast. Her pulse echoed louder than her shoes, a quiet thrum in her ears reminding her that while her steps were small, they were sacred.

She had been here before.

Not in this exact building, but certainly in this moment.

This *threshold*.

Where the air felt charged with the scent of transition. Like some strange alchemy of potential and panic. Where she could feel the invitation rising before her like mist, silent and invisible, but undeniably real. Where the fear wasn't of failure exactly, but of the audacity it took to imagine success.

Camryn stopped.

In front of her stood a single door. No fanfare. No flashing lights. Just a plain wooden door painted the color of molasses, framed in gold trim like a memory.

A nameplate rested just above eye level.

Engraved in small, serif font:

"Next Level: Authorized Entry Only"

Her eyebrows knit together. That word again.

Authorized.

Like so many places before, permission was implied but not promised.

She looked for a handle. A button. A keypad. Anything.

But the door was smooth. Seamless.

No handle.

No welcome mat.

No instructions.

Just silence.

Her stomach tightened.

Was this some kind of test?

Had she come to the wrong place?

Was she even supposed to be here?

Camryn looked back down the hallway.

Empty.

The air felt still, too still. The kind of still that made you want to lower your voice even when you were alone.

She knocked once.

No answer.

She waited. Knocked again.

Still nothing.

Camryn pressed her palm against the cool wood, half expecting it to swing open with a creak, half expecting it to reject her touch. It did neither. It simply stood, unmoved. Impenetrable. Passive in its power.

A rush of old doubts flooded in.

Maybe I'm not ready. Perhaps I'm not enough. Maybe this wasn't for me after all.

She whispered into the silence, more to herself than the door:

"I guess I'm not meant to go through."

Her voice sounded too small. Like a whisper wrapped in apology.

She took a step back.

Then, she heard it.

Not from a speaker. Not from the walls. Not from behind the door.

But from somewhere deep inside her chest.

A knowing.

A voice she had buried under years of deference and deflection.

"You keep waiting for someone to let you in, but this one's yours to open."

She froze.

Her fingers curled slowly into her palm, and there, as if it had always been there, was a key.

Simple. Smooth. Slightly warm. As light as breath and heavy with meaning.

How long had she been holding it?

How many times had she looked for access, never realizing the authority had always been in her hand?

Camryn looked back at the door. Still no handle. No keyhole. No hinges in sight.

She stood still for a moment, the hallway humming behind her, memory rising in waves.

She remembered:

- Being the first in her family to earn a graduate degree but still second-guessing her salary negotiations
- Speaking up in meetings only to be talked over
- Coaching colleagues on cultural humility while privately wondering when it would be her turn to be seen beyond her resilience

She had always been taught to wait.

To be polite.

To earn her way in.

But this door?

This wasn't about credentials.

This was a mirror.

She stepped forward.

And with one fluid motion, she lifted the key, not to *unlock*, but to *claim*.

She pressed it to the door's center.

Not forcefully. Not frantically.

Just *firmly*.

Intentionally.

The moment the key touched the wood, something shifted.

Not with sound or spectacle.

The door didn't creak open.

It dissolved.

Disintegrated into the air like mist, like illusion, like the lies she'd been told about what it takes to rise.

Behind the door was not what she expected.

There was no stage. No boardroom. No rows of chairs or shining name placards.

No applause.

No gatekeepers.

No spreadsheet to prove her worth.

There was only a room.

Small. Still. Sacred.

At the center of it stood a table; circular, like community. On it sat a mirror and a journal. Next to it, there was a single chair.

The walls were unadorned, perfect for soft beams of natural light pouring in from a skylight above, illuminating the space like divine approval.

It was not an arrival.

It was an **invitation**.

Camryn stepped in, her breath caught between awe and aching.

The mirror reflected her fully, not filtered, not posed, not influenced by someone else's gaze.

She saw it all:

- The shadows beneath her eyes from late nights and early meetings
- The curl of her lip that reminded her of her grandmother's strength
- The dimple she never noticed except when she was truly at peace

She was tired.

And radiant.

Scared and sacred.

She moved toward the table and sat, the chair cradling her with surprising comfort.

The journal was open to a blank page.

The pen beside it shimmered; not with ink, but with possibility.

She picked it up and began to write.

"I'm done waiting. I give myself permission."

And she meant every word.

Permission:

- To say no without explanation
- To say yes without guilt
- To leave tables where she's only expected to clap and not build
- To cry when she's moved and not feel unprofessional
- To rise even if no one cheers
- To *rest* and still be worthy

Each word was written as if in a ritual. Each sentence a breaking of chains.

She kept writing.

She wrote about the times she shrank herself to make others comfortable.

About the ways she learned to code-switch so fluently, she once forgot her own voice.

About how she confused survival for strategy.

And how *this...* this sacred space of clarity was the leadership no one taught her.

When she was done, she placed the pen beside the journal and laid the key gently on top of the page, as if sealing a covenant with herself.

She didn't cry.

But she *felt* everything.

The years she spent trying to prove herself.

The moments she nearly quit.

The dreams she shelved until "the time was right."

And finally, the quiet echo of her own voice, now unshackled:

"I am not the applicant.

I am the architect."

The room shimmered, not visibly, but spiritually.

Something had broken.

And something had begun.

Camryn stood.

She walked to the threshold where the door used to be.

Behind her: no fanfare. Ahead of her: no roadmap.

But beneath her feet?

Solid ground. Built by her own becoming.

And somewhere, on another floor, another hallway, another woman stood in front of her own door.

She wouldn't see Camryn there.

But she'd feel her.

She'd feel the key warming in her palm.

The whispers of ancestors rising in her bones.

The permission passed down like a torch.

And she would bravely step into who she was always meant to be.

AUTHOR'S REFLECTION: YOU DON'T NEED PERMISSION

The next level isn't something you earn with applause.

It's something you *access* when you stop asking for permission.

You don't need a door to open for you.

You *are* the threshold.

You Don't Need It, But Here It Is Anyway

If there's one thing I wish someone had handed me at the beginning of my leadership journey, it's this:

"You're allowed."

You're allowed to lead differently.

You're allowed to be emotional *and* strategic.

You're allowed to show up as your whole self, not just your résumé.

You're allowed to speak with clarity, even if it makes people uncomfortable.

You're allowed to say **no**.

You're allowed to say **yes** to things that stretch you.

You don't need to ask anyone's permission to become the woman you already are inside. But just in case you've been waiting for a sign, here it is:

Your Permission Slip (Print It. Post It. Live It.)

Dear Self,

You have permission to lead with love and authority.

You have permission to change your mind as you evolve.

You have permission to rest, retreat, and recharge.

You have permission to take up space in every room, in every way.

You have permission to say:

"I don't know."

"I need support."

"This doesn't serve me anymore."

You have permission to start over, even if others are watching.

You have permission to bring all of who you are:

- Your faith
- Your culture
- Your fire
- Your softness
- Your full humanity

You have permission to release shame.

You have permission to release guilt.

You have permission to release the version of you that only survived, and embrace the version of you that can *thrive*.

You are not too much. You are not too late. You are not alone.

Love, *You.*

REFLECTION PROMPT FOR THE READER:

What do you need to give yourself permission to do, feel, or become right now?

_____

_____

_____

_____

What false beliefs or outdated rules are you ready to unlearn?

_____

_____

_____

_____

How would you lead differently if you genuinely believed you were already enough?

_____

_____

_____

_____

CHAPTER 10
CAMRYN'S STORY: *THE PEBBLES AND THE JAR*

The jar sat in the center of her desk.

Glass. Wide. Empty, except for three large, smooth stones nestled at the bottom.

Camryn didn't remember where she first heard the analogy. A professor, maybe? Or a retreat facilitator? It didn't matter. The metaphor had lodged itself in her spirit and stayed there.

She'd carried it in her heart.

Today, she made it literal.

She had placed three big pebbles into the jar that morning:

Family. Health. Purpose.

Then she filled it with the rest: colored marbles to represent work, email, social media, board meetings, grocery lists, unread texts, unread books, deferred dreams.

And even though the jar looked full…

There was still room for sand.

Tiny grains: other people's expectations, unspoken guilt, unresolved grief, interruptions, good ideas with no boundaries, well-meaning invitations she didn't have the energy to accept.

She watched the sand slip through the cracks and settle in.

It almost overflowed.

Almost.

Camryn leaned back in her chair, staring at it, breath low and deep.

She thought about how many times she'd tried to pour her life in reverse, how she had packed in obligations first and hoped there would be room left for joy. For healing. For herself.

There never was.

Not until she named her non-negotiables.

Not until she made peace with disappointing people who expected her to be endlessly available.

Not until she realized that *every "yes" costs something*, and her peace was no longer on clearance.

The shift didn't happen overnight.

It started small.

She began to put her phone on do not disturb in the evening.

She let emails wait until morning, even when they screamed urgency.

She said no to panels that felt like performative diversity plays.

She chose sleep over another round of edits.

She took walks without podcasts, letting silence speak for once.

She let her body lead instead of her calendar.

Camryn started blocking off full days for herself, no meetings, no calls. Just creation. Rest. Reflection. The kind of soul-tending she used to think she had to earn.

She realized that success wasn't about doing more.

It was more discernment.

One day, an intern walked into her office and looked at the jar.

"What's that for?" he asked, curious.

Camryn smiled and held the jar up with pride.

"It's a reminder," she said. "That the big stuff has to go in first. Or it won't fit at all."

He nodded slowly. "Like your time with family?"

"Exactly," she whispered, with an affirming head nod. "That's one of the big ones."

Later that night, Camryn journaled by candlelight.

No agenda. No goal. Just clarity.

She wrote:

My life is not a list. It's a legacy.

And it would not be dictated by the loudest voice in the room.

The next morning, she walked into her office and moved the jar to the shelf where she could see it every day.

The big pebbles still sat at the bottom, steady and sure.

And above them?

Only what fits.

AUTHOR'S REFLECTION: HOW I STAY ANCHORED WHILE THE WORLD PULLS ON ME

Leadership will stretch you.

Visibility will test you.

Purpose will pull on parts of you that aren't fully healed yet.

So if you're going to rise, you need practices that *hold you* while you do.

These aren't hacks. They're *soul infrastructure*, rituals that remind you of who you are when the world tries to make you forget.

Here are a few that have kept me centered on the days I felt powerful, and especially on the days I didn't.

1. Quiet Mornings With My Mirror

I don't rush into the world anymore.

I spend time with myself first, face to face, eye to eye.

No makeup. No mask. Just me and the woman I'm becoming.

Sometimes I speak affirmations. Sometimes I cry. But I always *see* myself.

Mirror Prompt:

What does the woman in the mirror need to hear today?

2. Journaling With Intention

My journal is my sacred container.

It holds my fears, my vision, my prayers, and my wildest dreams.

I don't write for performance. I write for clarity. To process. To purge. To remember.

Journal Prompts:

- What am I carrying today that I need to set down?
- What truth am I avoiding?
- Where am I being called to expand, even if it scares me?

3. Spiritual Anchoring

For me, it's prayer.

Scripture.

Sermons.

Songs that shift the atmosphere in my soul.

I need a source bigger than my goals. I need *God* in the details.

Practice: Create a "Becoming" playlist, music that reminds you of your strength, your softness, and your calling.

4. Body Movement as Worship and Warfare

Some days it's walking.

Some days it's dancing.

Some days it's stretching through the tension.

I move not to chase beauty, but to embody power.

To remind myself that I'm alive, and this body is my home.

Check-In:

What does my body need from me today: gentleness, strength, stillness, or release?

5. Saturday Alignment

Once a week, I pause to check in:

- What drained me?
- What filled me?
- What did I say yes to that I didn't mean?
- What do I want the new week to feel like?

This is where I come back to my mission, not my momentum.

Try it: Block 30 minutes every weekend for stillness, strategy, and soul work.

Your Practices Are the Blueprint

You don't have to do all of this.

You don't have to get it "right."

You just have to return to yourself.

Because the most powerful leader is not the one with the loudest voice, it's the one who stays rooted in truth, *even when no one's watching.*

REFLECTION PROMPT FOR THE READER:

What daily or weekly practices do you need to create a life you don't have to escape from?

_____

_____

_____

_____

Where can you make space to see, hear, and hold yourself?

_____

_____

_____

_____

PART

Three

THE RISING

CHAPTER 11
CAMRYN'S STORY: RISING STRONG

Camryn closed the door behind her more gently than she wanted to.

If she'd shut it the way she *felt*, it would've echoed through the whole building, rattling picture frames, setting off car alarms, maybe even drawing someone out to ask if she was okay.

But nobody was coming. Not today.

She slid down the back of the door until she was on the floor of her apartment, back pressed to the wood, palms flat on the cold tile. Her bag slumped beside her. She didn't even take off her shoes.

Everything felt… heavy.

Not the kind of heavy that comes from a single hard meeting, a missed deadline, or a misunderstood email. This was the kind of weight that came from the accumulation of expectations, of code-switching, of biting her tongue in rooms that demanded her labor but denied her leadership.

She realized that even her best efforts to remind herself to remain strong and resilient had their limits.

It had been a month of Mondays. A year of pretending. A career of carrying.

Camryn tilted her head back until it knocked softly against the door and closed her eyes. She wasn't crying. Not yet. But the silence pressed against her like a weighted blanket.

And still, there was that whisper again, the one that had been rising louder each week.

Something has to change.

She didn't get up right away.

She sat on the floor until her legs tingled and her phone buzzed somewhere deep in her bag. She ignored it. She didn't want to perform gratitude today. Didn't want to be reminded of her blessings when she felt buried beneath them.

Was that selfish? Maybe.

But what Camryn had learned, after years of burnout disguised as productivity, was that ignoring the signs didn't make them go away. In fact, that's how she'd ended up here in the first place: trying to outwork a system designed to drain her.

She was tired of proving she belonged in spaces that didn't deserve her presence.

The next morning, Camryn stood in front of her bathroom mirror brushing her teeth, staring at the woman looking back at her.

Puffy eyes. Wrinkled blouse. A tight smile that didn't quite reach her eyes.

She whispered to the mirror, toothbrush still in hand:

"This can't be it."

Who Camryn Really Was

Underneath the title, the business card, and the carefully curated LinkedIn bio, Camryn was a woman built from faith and fight.

She was the daughter of a mother who turned scraps into Sunday feasts. A sister to women who stitched joy out of pain and passed it around like an offering plate during Sunday service. A friend to a tribe who reminded her daily that her voice mattered more than her job title.

She was soft-spoken, but not small. Kind, but not passive. And she was done pretending that navigating toxic workplaces was a skill to be proud of.

Camryn wasn't fragile. But she was tired.

And tired wasn't the enemy.

Denial was.

The Quiet Collapse

The week had unraveled slowly.

Her boss had dismissed her suggestion in a meeting, only for it to be praised when someone else rephrased it: someone louder, and Whiter, and male.

Her calendar had become a graveyard of back-to-back meetings that never ended in decisions.

Her gifts, her vision, her emotional intelligence, and her ability to build bridges were being minimized as "nice to have" rather than what they were: strategic imperatives.

And every time she opened her laptop, her chest tightened; not from fear, but from misalignment.

It wasn't that she didn't want to work.

She just didn't want to betray herself to do it.

That following Saturday, Camryn did something radical.

She turned off every notification on her phone.

She brewed her favorite tea.

She climbed back into bed in the middle of the day, wrapped herself in her grandmother's quilt, and let herself *do nothing* without guilt.

At first, her mind protested:

You should be doing something.

You're wasting time.

You're falling behind.

You're not strong enough.

But beneath the noise was something quieter.

Something wiser.

A truth that had been waiting patiently beneath the rubble of burnout.

You're not broken. You're just exhausted from carrying what was never yours to hold.

Camryn didn't quit her job that Monday.

But she did quit performing wellness for the comfort of others.

She stopped answering emails after 7 PM.

She reclaimed her lunch breaks.

She began writing again: journal entries at first, then blog posts, and finally pages that might someday become a book.

She didn't announce a grand pivot. She just began to reorient herself around truth.

Her truth.

She stopped saying "yes" to things that drained her, even if they came with visibility or a seat at the table.

Because what good was a seat if you couldn't speak freely from it?

People often mistook Camryn's calm for compliance.

But her silence wasn't a weakness.

It was a strategy.

She was learning when to speak, when to rest, when to resist, and when to walk away entirely.

She realized that strength wasn't measured by how long you stayed in toxic spaces.

Sometimes, strength was in the exit.

Sometimes resilience wasn't about pushing through. It was about stepping back to build something new.

Camryn didn't talk much about her faith at work.

It wasn't "professional."

But in the quiet hours of the morning, with the sun peeking through her blinds, her journal open, and her coffee warm in her hands, faith met her like an old friend.

God didn't need her to be impressive.

He needed her to be *honest*.

She wrote prayers in the margins of her planner and scribbled scripture on sticky notes. Lit candles and cried when no one was watching.

She didn't need a pulpit.

She needed permission to believe she could begin again.

The job didn't change.

But she did.

And that changed everything.

She started having brave conversations with her boss, with herself, and with God.

Some of them ended in understanding.

Some in boundaries.

Some in redirection.

She started dreaming again, not escape-type fantasies, but legacy-level plans. Ideas that included peace, purpose, and ownership.

She realized she didn't need to burn it all down.

She just needed to light up the parts of herself she had dimmed.

Camryn began keeping a note in her phone.

She called it her "Bounce-Back Blueprint."

It wasn't fancy. Just reminders for when the fog rolled in:

Name what's true. You are not crazy. This is hard.

Get in your body. Go for a walk. Breathe. Hydrate.

Stop the noise. Mute the world before it mutes *you.*

Talk to God before you talk to your fear.

Remember who you are. Write it down if you forget.

Plan your way out. Not out of fear. Out of alignment.

Rest like it's sacred. Because it is.

Camryn didn't wake up one day fully healed or entirely clear.

But she woke up every day a little more honest.

She became a woman who no longer needed to *convince* people of her value.

She became a woman who stopped apologizing for needing joy, not just achievement.

She became a woman who didn't wait for permission to pivot.

She became her own rescuer.

Camryn stood in her kitchen one evening, making dinner, soft music playing, windows open to the sounds of the city.

She thought about the months she had spent dragging herself through days that didn't deserve her energy, and she whispered to herself, a benediction and a declaration:

"I'm still here. But I'm not the same."

And for the first time in a long time, she accepted who she was becoming and the inevitability of change.

AUTHOR'S REFLECTION: AT THE EDGE OF AGAIN

Starting over is not glamorous. It's gritty.

It looks like brushing your teeth in silence and whispering "this can't be it" to your own reflection.

It looks like rereading your calendar, your résumé, your journal, trying to make sense of how you got so far from yourself while doing everything "right."

It feels like both exhaustion and clarity are showing up in the same breath.

I've been there—the space between breakdown and breakthrough.

That sacred space where you know you're not okay, but you also know you're not lost.

Floorboards of your life creaking under the weight of your own self-denial. When you stop showing up for the performance and finally ask, "What would it look like to show up for me?"

It's not a clean pivot. It's not always a clear path.

Sometimes, it starts in your bones before it ever hits your lips.

A subtle shift in your spirit. An internal rebellion.

That kind of bounce back doesn't begin with grand declarations.

It begins when you finally take your foot off the gas and say:

"I'm allowed to pause. I'm allowed to choose again."

Not because the world gave you permission.

But because your soul refused to keep settling.

Camryn didn't just reclaim her time. She reclaimed her tenderness.

And if I'm honest, I've had to do the same.

I've had to remember that real strength isn't in how loud you roar, but how clearly you listen... to yourself, to God, to the quiet knowing that you're being called into something more honest.

Sometimes resilience isn't climbing back up.

Sometimes it's staying down long enough to ask why you were climbing in the first place.

And when you get the answer?

You don't run back into the fire.

You rise slower, softer, surer.

You stop editing your truth to fit into a room that was never built for your fullness.

You start designing spaces that reflect your actual power.

Not the performance.

Not the potential.

The present you.

So if you're standing at the edge of a fresh start, shaking, praying, grieving, remembering, know this:

You are not back at zero.

You are standing on sacred ground paved by every version of you who kept going.

Every lesson. Every detour. Every quiet no. Every exhausted, yes.

You are not weak for needing rest.

You are wise for choosing alignment.

Start again.

But this time, start from wholeness.

REFLECTION PROMPT FOR THE READER:

Where in your life have you been trying to "tough it out" in a space that no longer fits who you're becoming?

What does resilience look like when it's rooted in rest, truth, and faith, not just endurance?

What would your "Bounce-Back Blueprint" include if you made one today? What's missing that your soul needs?

CHAPTER 12
CAMRYN'S STORY: THE EXIT THAT SAVED HER

The signs didn't come in a flash of drama.

They came in whispers.

At first, Camryn ignored them, as most strong women do. A furrowed brow here, a breath held too long there. That low-grade exhaustion that no amount of sleep could fix. The way her name sounded when called in meetings was sharp and tight, like a command rather than an invitation.

It didn't feel like a breaking. Not at first.

It felt like shrinking.

Meetings where her ideas were hijacked mid-sentence.

Reports she poured herself into barely skimmed.

Performance praised in private, dismissed in public.

The same microaggressions, cloaked in professionalism.

And worst of all? The way she'd started gaslighting herself.

Maybe I *am* too sensitive.

Maybe that *was* just a joke.

Maybe I *should* be grateful just to be here.

Gratitude had become a leash, a velvet rope around her neck. The kind that looked like opportunity from the outside but felt like suffocation every time she tried to speak her truth.

The final version of herself in that space sat in a tiny office with no windows. She noticed it one day, the metaphor screaming at her. No windows. No view. Just the glow of artificial lights above and the flickering exhaustion in her chest.

She remembered bringing plants to work.

Little signs of life; succulents, ivy, hearty plants that didn't require much.

But still, they all died, one by one.

The light wasn't real enough for them to thrive.

Neither was the environment for her.

Not Burnt Out-*Dried Up*

Quiet quitting wasn't a trend for Camryn.

It was survival.

It wasn't some passive rebellion.

It was a sacred act of preservation.

She began to move differently.

Still punctual, still excellent. But no longer performative.

She stopped staying late to fix messes she didn't create.

She stopped volunteering for tasks that didn't feed her spirit.

She stopped overexplaining. Over justifying. Overgiving.

She stopped shrinking her light just to make others feel more comfortable in their shadows.

Instead, she did her job. And she left.

And when they noticed her pulling back?

They called it attitude.

They called it distance.

They called it a decline.

But never once did they call it what it really was: a woman outgrowing her cage.

Camryn didn't wait for permission.

She didn't storm out.

She pivoted.

Softly. Powerfully.

With clarity, not cruelty.

She kept it quiet, not out of shame, but out of strategy.

Because she knew they'd try to convince her to stay for their benefit, not hers.

The pivot began in small, sacred steps.

She stopped taking work calls on her lunch break.

She walked outside at noon, face turned toward the sun.

She prayed in the restroom stall.

She wrote affirmations in the margins of her notebooks.

She downloaded coaching worksheets and business podcasts during her commute.

It wasn't that she hated her job.

It's that the job no longer honored the woman she was becoming.

One evening, Camryn stayed late; not for work, but to pack her office quietly.

She didn't announce it.

She didn't owe them spectacle.

She deserved stillness.

She boxed her things slowly: the framed quote from her grandmother, the worn-out mousepad with "You Got This!" printed in peeling gold, the stack of leadership books with dog-eared pages and highlighter ink still fresh.

Then she sat down in the chair for the last time and looked at the mirror behind the door.

Not the kind you see your makeup in.

The kind that reveals you're becoming.

Her reflection was worn, but not defeated.

There were bags under her eyes, but not over her dreams.

She whispered, "You don't need to prove anything anymore."

And for the first time in months, her body believed her.

There's grief in letting go.

Leaving didn't feel triumphant.

It felt tender.

You don't just walk away from a job.

You walk away from your inner child, who begged for stability.

You walk away from the version of you that fought to be seen.

You walk away from the dream you were sold, that if you work twice as hard, you'll finally belong.

She mourned that dream.

Mourned it in the car on the drive home.

Mourned it in the bathtub that night, hot water loosening tears that had stayed trapped behind her eyes for far too long.

But beneath the grief, there was something more profound:

Peace.

She became unapologetically unavailable.

Camryn didn't announce her liberation on LinkedIn.

She just *left*.

And when the emails started...

the "Can we chat?", the "Where did you go?", the "Let's catch up sometime!"

She replied with gratitude, but not obligation.

Because when you quietly quit, the real quitting isn't about the job.

It's about quitting the performative survival.

She became unavailable for:

- Code-switching until her throat was sore
- Playing "team player" while carrying the whole damn team
- Being everyone's "go-to" until she had nowhere to go for herself
- Fixing systems designed to break her
- Performing gratitude while internally screaming

And what she made space for instead?

- Soft mornings
- Creative ideas
- Coaching calls that lit her up
- Sleep. Real, full, undisturbed sleep
- Joy without explanation
- A community that saw her clearly

The New Sound of Success

Success started sounding different.

It wasn't applause, bonuses, or being "included."

It was quiet. Steady. True.

It was her breath not catching when her phone rang.

It was walking into rooms where she could tell the truth without translation.

It was lighting a candle in the morning and praying without rushing.

It was hearing her name and not flinching.

Camryn didn't just walk away.

She walked *toward* something.

Toward alignment.

Toward breath.

Toward joy without burnout.

Toward a purpose that didn't ask her to abandon herself to access it.

And when she tells her story now?

She doesn't say, "I quit my job."

She says, "I remembered who I was."

Because quiet quitting wasn't a failure.

It was freedom. It was resilience

The world likes resilience when it looks like pushing through.

Like holding it all together.

Like being everything to everyone.

But Camryn's resilience was a sacred refusal.

Refusal to play small.

Refusal to chase worth.

Refusal to pretend survival was enough.

She was resilient *when she walked away.*

Resilient *when she whispered no more.*

Resilient *when she chose peace over performance.*

The Journal Page That Sealed It

Weeks later, Camryn sat at her kitchen table, sunlight pouring in, tea steaming beside her, a pen in her hand, and a knowing in her chest.

She opened her journal, the one she kept hidden in the bottom drawer of her office desk.

And she wrote a few words before she drafted an open letter to women she may never know:

I left the room that asked me to abandon myself to belong.

I stopped dancing for crumbs and started baking my own cake.

I did not leave in rage. I left in reverence; for my voice, my vision, my vitality.

Quiet quitting wasn't me giving up.

It was me waking up.

A Love Letter to Every Woman on the Edge

If you're reading this and feeling the weight

The slow suffocation of being silenced in spaces you've outgrown

The ache of knowing you are made for more, but scared to leap

The guilt of not being "grateful enough"

The fear of starting over…

Let my exit be your mirror.

Let it be your permission slip.

Let it be your reminder that:

You do not need to burn out to be valuable.

You do not need to explain your exhaustion to deserve rest.

You do not need their applause to validate your exhale.

You do not need to stay where your spirit is starving.

Your quiet exit can be the loudest affirmation of your worth.

Love, Cam

Reclamation

Camryn placed her journal on the table, exhaled deeply, and smiled.

Not the smile they trained her to wear.

But the one that blooms only when a woman chooses herself fully.

The tea had gone cold.

The sun was setting.

And for the first time in years, she felt whole.

She didn't conquer the world.

She reclaimed herself.

And sometimes, that's the greatest victory of all.

AUTHOR'S REFLECTION: WHAT THEY NEVER TELL YOU

They never tell you that sometimes quitting is holy.

They never tell you that silence can be a strategy.

They never tell you that the loudest "no" you ever say might come without words.

They don't tell you that peace has a sound, and it's the sound of your own breath when you're not bracing anymore.

No one teaches you how to leave the room without performing a scene.

No one claps when you walk away from the thing that used to be your dream, but now feels like a slow suffocation wrapped in a paycheck.

They don't prepare you for the kind of grief that comes with choosing yourself. The ache of releasing a version of you who tried so hard to belong. The quiet ceremony of mourning stability while reaching for freedom.

But let me tell you what I now know:

Leaving isn't always running.

Sometimes, it's returning.

Returning to your voice. Your rhythm. Your alignment.

It's remembering that you never needed to earn rest.

That burnout isn't a badge of honor.

That resilience doesn't always look like pushing through; it can also look like backing out with grace.

I used to think that "quiet quitting" meant failure.

That if I wasn't fighting to be seen, I wasn't doing enough.

But what I've come to understand is this,

There is nothing louder than a woman reclaiming her peace.

Nothing more powerful than walking away *without apology*.

Camryn's story is not just a reflection; it's a mirror.

And if you're reading this while navigating your own exit, whether physical or spiritual, know this:

You are not lost. You are locating yourself.

You're not broken. You're being *rebuilt*.

You don't have to stay anywhere that demands you shrink to fit.

You don't have to explain why you're tired.

You don't have to make your healing digestible for people who benefited from your burnout.

Your evolution is not up for debate.

And the exit?

It isn't the end.

It's the invitation to the next chapter.

REFLECTION PROMPT FOR THE READER:

Where in your life are you still performing?

_____

_____

_____

_____

What would it look like to stop performing and start honoring your truth?

_____

_____

_____

_____

What have you outgrown, but are afraid to release?

_____

_____

_____

_____

Do you notice tension, anxiety, exhaustion, silence, or even physical illness in certain environments?

_____

_____

_____

_____

What would "leaving well" look like for you?

_____

_____

_____

_____

CHAPTER 13
CAMRYN'S STORY: NOT STARTING FROM SCRATCH

Camryn stood in her living room surrounded by half-packed boxes, the scent of lavender from the candle she'd just blown out still hanging in the air. It was a familiar scene, her third move in five years. But this time, it didn't feel like retreat.

It felt like a *release*.

A closing without collapse. A beginning without begging.

There was no chaos this time. No frantic search for the nearest escape hatch. No disgruntled resignation letter drafted at midnight. Just a quiet, settled knowing in her bones:

I'm not starting over. I'm starting with wisdom.

Quitting wasn't all rebellion. It was part revolution and a larger part self-preservation.

People love to say it.

"Back to square one."

As if everything you've lived through resets the moment you choose a new direction. As if the tears, the breakthroughs, the promotions, the pivots, the heartbreaks, the silent wins, the late-night prayers, all of it disappears just because you've decided to change course.

But Camryn knew better.

She had *earned* her pivots.

She didn't stumble into this moment. She'd been gathering tools. Insight. Language. Discernment. Authority.

Every misstep and miracle shaped the woman she now saw in the mirror.

She wasn't starting over.

She was building from the deep knowing that only comes when you've walked through the fire and *lived* to testify.

Camryn was never the type to fake it until she made it.

She didn't believe in pretending to be unbothered or acting like her timeline hadn't shifted. She believed in *truth-telling*. In owning the ache without apology.

And truthfully?

The last few seasons had *tested* her.

Tested her patience. Her optimism. Her commitment to herself.

She'd worked in rooms that shrunk her. Built teams she had to walk away from. Answered to leaders who never really *saw* her.

And still, she kept showing up.

Because she had dreams that outlived her circumstances.

Because she believed that integrity was a quiet form of rebellion.

Because even when her plans unraveled, her purpose never did.

There's a grief that comes with leaving something you once prayed for.

Camryn felt that.

She remembered applying for the job she was now walking away from. She remembered begging God for a chance. For provision. For a way out of what she thought was rock bottom.

She'd gotten it.

And now… she was choosing to lay it down.

Not because it was all bad. But because she had outgrown the version of herself that needed to prove she belonged in that space.

She didn't need to prove anymore.

She needed to *build*.

Something that wouldn't crumble every time she stopped performing.

Camryn made a list.

Not of regrets, but of **receipts**.

- Teams she led that exceeded expectations.
- Community partnerships she'd initiated from scratch.
- Hard conversations she navigated with grace.
- Boundaries she held that once terrified her.
- Messages from mentees whose lives she'd quietly impacted.
- Projects she delivered under pressure.
- Rooms she entered and left better than she found them.

She didn't need accolades. She had evidence.

The world might call it starting over. She called it **starting *from***.

From wisdom. From clarity. From conviction. From capacity.

Camryn didn't hate that job.

But she was no longer in love with it.

It felt like trying to breathe in a room with no windows. Like putting on a coat that used to fit but now feels stiff at the shoulders and tight at the waist.

Letting go wasn't impulsive. It was *sacred*.

She spent time discerning her next step.

She talked to mentors. She sat in prayer. She asked herself hard questions:

"Am I still growing here?"

"Do I trust myself to lead from alignment, not fear?"

"What am I holding onto that no longer holds me?"

Eventually, the answer came softly but with strength.

It's time.

One of the most profound shifts Camryn experienced was this:

She no longer felt the need to *earn* rest, respect, or recognition.

She realized how many years she'd spent in rooms trying to be palatable, promotable, perfect.

How she'd treated her résumé like an apology; like she needed to overcompensate for her presence.

No more.

She was done with proving.

She was ready for planting.

Camryn's next season wasn't going to be about hustle.

It was going to be about *harvesting*.

Tending to what had been buried.

Reclaiming the parts of herself she'd ignored in pursuit of a title.

She began to write again, not for work, but for healing.

She started mapping out a business idea she'd shelved for years.

She said yes to speaking engagements that aligned with her *voice*, not just her expertise.

She took walks in the middle of the day.

She napped on purpose.

She read books that didn't come with action steps.

She gave herself *permission* to rebuild without rushing.

Camryn often thought about how people described transitions.

"Starting from scratch."

But what she'd come to understand was this:

Every pivot had a blueprint.

Every detour carried data.

Every fall revealed something sacred.

She wasn't guessing anymore. She was designing.

She knew how to advocate.

How to interview from power.

How to spot red flags before signing a contract.

How to choose collaborators instead of saviors.

How to build without bleeding.

She didn't need to ask, "Am I good enough?"

She started asking, "Does this align with who I am becoming?"

A New Definition of Success

In the past, success looked like promotions, pay raises, and plaques.

Now?

Success looked like **freedom**.

The freedom to say no without guilt.

The freedom to be Black and fully brilliant.

The freedom to rest without explaining.

The freedom to speak without shrinking.

Camryn decided to define success on her own terms:

Joy. Integrity. Purpose. Peace.

If an opportunity didn't bring at least three of those, it wasn't hers.

Some people didn't understand.

They'd ask if she was sure.

They would remind her of the job market. The economy. The risks.

They might praise her courage... with a side of concern.

But Camryn didn't need everyone to get it.

She just needed to remember:

I am not lost. I am choosing a different path.

Camryn prayed for grace in the in-between.

There were sure to be hard days.

Days when she questioned everything.

When fear whispered, "What if this doesn't work?"

When comparison knocked on her door, holding Instagram posts of former colleagues with curated smiles and corner offices.

But on those days, she would be sure to slow down.

She would cook. Call a friend. Pray. Light a candle. Take a nap. Play music way too loud. Dance barefoot in her living room. Re-read her journal entries. Walk under the sky.

She would give herself grace.

Because starting again doesn't mean you failed.

It means you refused to settle.

One night, curled up with tea and her favorite throw blanket, Camryn whispered a prayer.

"God, I don't know what's next. But I trust what You placed in me."

And for the first time in months, she felt peace settle in her chest.

Not because she had all the answers.

But because she had finally stopped betraying herself to make others comfortable.

Camryn is no longer afraid of pivots.

She's not afraid to walk away from the good for the *right*.

She doesn't see blank pages as failure.

She sees them as **freedom.**

She's not rebuilding.

She's **reclaiming.**

She's not asking for a seat at the table.

She's building a house with **room for others**.

Because what she's constructing now?

It's rooted in truth.

And truth always holds.

AUTHOR'S REFLECTION: BUILDING FROM WHAT'S BEEN GATHERED

Starting again used to terrify me.

There was a time when the very idea of changing direction made my stomach tighten. I'd grown up believing that stability equaled success, and any shift, even one guided by God, wisdom, or exhaustion, meant I hadn't gotten something right the first time. That I had miscalculated. Mis-stepped. Missed my moment.

But what I've learned, painfully and beautifully, is this:

Starting over is rarely about beginning from nothing.

It's about beginning from knowing.

From the lessons we didn't want but needed.

From the boundaries we finally honored.

From the clarity that only fatigue can teach you.

From the courage that grows quietly in the dark.

The world romanticizes fresh starts: vision boards, new planners, color-coordinated calendars, as if the rebirth is clean, crisp, and organized. I love those tools myself. But the truth is far less glamorous and far more real: the best beginnings are born from endings that taught us too much to ignore.

And that was the truth living in my own chest.

I wasn't empty. I wasn't erased.

I wasn't at square one.

I was simply at the next chapter of who I could finally admit I was becoming.

I had tools now. Tools I didn't have when I first said yes to rooms that shrunk me, roles that drained me, or expectations that were never mine to carry. I had language now, not the kind built for professionalism, but the kind rooted in honesty, boundaries, discernment, and truth.

I had history now, receipts, really, of all the moments I thought would break me but ended up building muscles I never knew I needed. Muscles of self-trust. Muscles of intuition. Muscles of "no, this isn't for me." Muscles that could finally lift the dream I had been too afraid to pick up before.

And so this time, I chose to see myself as someone who wasn't simply beginning again, but someone who was building from the ashes, the lessons, the clarity, the scars, and the victories that had shaped me.

Because the truth is:

Every pivot I survived had a purpose.

Every door I closed left me with a key.

Every fall handed me a blueprint.

Every "not yet" prepared me for "now."

I stopped asking myself, "Why didn't it work out?"

And started asking, "What did I gain that I didn't know I needed?"

That shift from shame to stewardship changed everything.

The pressure to start over melted away.

And in its place rose a quiet strength.

A calm I hadn't felt in years.

A confidence that didn't need to be performed.

I no longer felt the urge to prove myself in rooms that couldn't honor me.

I no longer needed validation to feel valuable.

I no longer felt guilty for choosing the path that aligned with who I actually was, not the version I thought others wanted.

This time, I am building from:

Wisdom earned through fire.

Joy I no longer postpone.

Discernment sharpened by disappointment.

Faith strengthened by every unanswered prayer that later reveals its purpose.

Authority rooted in lived experience, not borrowed confidence.

Peace that cost too much to put back down.

I carry every woman I've been:

The one who hustled for worth,

The one who settled for breadcrumbs,

The one who fought to be seen,

The one who dimmed her light,

The one who lost herself and still kept going.

They are all here with me, not as reminders of failure, but as evidence of survival.

So no, I'm not starting over.

I am starting from fullness. From everything I gained when I thought I was losing.

I am building from alignment now.

From intentionality.

From softness.

From self-trust.

From God's timing, not mine.

And this time?

What I create will not crumble when I stop performing.

It will not shrink when I grow.

It will not demand that I abandon myself to sustain it.

It will rise with me. Because I am building it as the woman I've become, not the woman I was pretending to be.

If you, too, are standing at the edge of a new beginning, wondering if you have to go back to zero, hear me clearly:

You are not at zero.

You are at **wisdom.**

You are at **clarity.**

You are at **alignment.**

You are at **the next level of your becoming.**

Everything you've lived, survived, learned, and carried is coming with you.

You are not starting over; you are starting from the truth.

And truth always builds something that holds.

REFLECTION & DISCUSSION PROMPTS

What "starting over" moment in your life was really a "starting from wisdom" moment in disguise?

_____

_____

_____

_____

What tools, truths, or experiences are you carrying with you into your next chapter?

_____

_____

_____

_____

Are you making choices based on fear or based on alignment with who you're becoming?

_____

_____

_____

_____

What would it look like to stop proving and start planting in your life right now?

CHAPTER 14
CAMRYN'S STORY: WHEN IT FINALLY FEELS RIGHT

Camryn stood in front of the small brick building, coffee in one hand, a messenger bag slung across her chest, and the key to a door she never thought she'd open in the other.

It wasn't flashy. No glistening glass walls or private offices with leather chairs. Just an old, repurposed house in the heart of the city, on the edge of the same neighborhood where she used to catch the bus to her after-school job, walking past boarded-up storefronts and loose dogs chasing dreams and strangers alike.

But to her, this building was sacred ground.

This was the place where her work, the *real* work, was finally beginning.

She turned the key.

The scent of fresh paint and eucalyptus oil lingered in the air, mingling with the quiet hum of a small desk fan in the corner. Natural light poured in through the tall windows, hitting the gallery wall she'd just installed with pictures of women she admired; Black women, strong women, women who never got their flowers.

Angela. Toni. Shirley. Her mother.

Camryn inhaled slowly, then stepped inside, the wooden floors creaking beneath her boots. She ran her fingers across the surface of the handmade conference table she thrifted and refinished herself. She had bruised her knuckles and broken a few nails sanding that thing down, but something about making it her own felt like giving birth.

This space had been pieced together with borrowed money, relentless faith, and Pinterest boards full of color palettes that felt like joy. She remembered bringing in the big armchair for the reading nook in the back room. She sat in it every morning before the contractors arrived, sipping her tea and whispering the same prayer:

"Let this place be a refuge. Let it heal, not just others, but me too."

And now it was real.

She wasn't dreaming anymore.

It had taken years to get here.

Years of saying "one day" while showing up to jobs where her soul had to shrink to survive.

Of launching bold ideas in rooms where silence greeted her passion.

Of sitting through strategy meetings where the mission was profit, not people.

Years of being told she was "too much," and then, in the same breath, "not enough."

She'd played the game. Decorated the title. Polished the résumé. Earned the seat.

And yet, every day she climbed the corporate ladder, she could feel it:

This was not the summit she was made for.

The real work, her work, had always lived somewhere deeper.

Her new nonprofit wasn't about vanity metrics or performative partnerships. It wasn't about grants with golden strings or photos for the annual report.

It was about real change.

Camryn built a center for Black women navigating leadership, caregiving, and trauma recovery. A space for women who were both praised and overlooked. Who ran companies by day and collapsed on their kitchen floors at night.

Workshops. Coaching circles. Healing spaces. Art. Advocacy. Storytelling. Wraparound wellness.

Camryn knew the stats.

But this wasn't about statistics.

This was about *Sharonda*, who had a C-suite title but hadn't cried in five years because the last time she did, HR called her "unstable."

This was about *Denise*, the 65-year-old grandmother raising three kids after her daughter's incarceration, who had more wisdom in her pinky than most leadership consultants.

This was about *herself*, too. About reclaiming the parts of her identity she'd numbed with productivity and performance.

The space was *alive* with purpose.

And today?

It finally had a heartbeat.

Camryn didn't expect fireworks on day one. But she wasn't prepared for how deeply it would move her to see the first three women walk through her door.

They arrived one by one.

All different. But familiar. Black women in transition. Between jobs. Between dreams. Between breakdown and breakthrough.

They looked around the room as if trying to remember what breathing felt like.

Camryn greeted them with hugs, not handshakes. Warmth first. Business later.

She brewed coffee and tea in the back and invited them to take off their shoes if they wanted to. "We do ease in this space," she said.

When they sat in a circle, Camryn didn't launch into a welcome speech. She just asked a question:

"What part of you needs permission today?"

And then they began.

Not resumes. Not titles. Not affiliations.

Just stories.

Tears. Laughter. Testimonies.

And in that circle, Camryn felt her chest rise with triumph.

This is it.

This is why every "no" had been worth it.

Why the detours weren't mistakes, they were training.

Why the delay wasn't denial, it was *divine design.*

She stayed late that night.

The city dimmed outside her windows, streetlights flickering on one by one.

She kicked off her shoes and curled up in the chair with her journal.

The pages held the kind of exhaustion that didn't come from stress, but from *birthing a new thing.*

She wrote:

"I don't want to lead from my wounds anymore. I want to lead from my wisdom. I want to model what healing looks like. I want to create spaces where brilliance doesn't require burnout."

She thought of her nieces and nephews.

She thought about what it would mean for them to see their auntie doing what she was *called* to do, not just what she was *capable* of.

She thought of her younger self, the Camryn who used to take the long way home to avoid being seen in her hand-me-down clothes, embarrassed by things she had no personal control over.

What would that Camryn say now?

Would she recognize this woman?

Would she believe it?

People always talked about the struggle of starting a business.

And don't get her wrong, **it was hard.**

Camryn still had moments where she triple-checked the math in her QuickBooks file and prayed the grant money would clear before the rent was due.

But the emotional labor?

It was different now.

She wasn't contorting. She wasn't editing her light. She wasn't begging for belonging.

She had built something that *fit*.

It didn't steal from her; it *fed* her.

She didn't dread Mondays. She didn't hold her breath during team meetings. She didn't feel like she was playing dress-up in someone else's vision.

It was *hers*.

Every wall color. Every playlist. Every policy.

Her fingerprints. Her legacy.

The impact wasn't just in the programming. It was in the ripple effect.

Women started saying things they hadn't dared to say in years:

"I'm allowed to change my mind."

"I'm tired of settling."

"I deserve joy."

One woman, a nurse administrator, quit her job two months after a retreat at Camryn's center and started her own health consulting practice. Another created a grief group for Black women in ministry. A third decided to go back to school for art therapy at 52.

Camryn wasn't giving them answers.

She was giving them **mirrors**.

And mirrors? When clean, when true, when loving?

They are *revolutionary*.

It Doesn't Have to Hurt to Count

Camryn knew pain.

She knew survival.

She knew how to lead in crisis and push through burnout.

But now?

She was finally learning how to lead in peace.

In softness. In stillness. In ease.

It didn't mean she wasn't working hard.

But her work wasn't hollow.

It was honorable and fulfilling.

She no longer equated purpose with suffering.

She believed that joy was *also* a sign of alignment.

The systems were still flawed.

The world still required her to be twice as good.

She still had to fight for funding, visibility, and space.

But she wasn't waiting for the world to shift before she did.

She decided:

I will not shrink myself waiting for this world to become safer. I will become more whole and build what I need despite it.

That kind of courage was contagious.

When people asked what she did now, Camryn didn't list titles.

She said:

"I build spaces where Black women can come home to themselves."

And then she'd smile; wide, unapologetic, and free.

Because for the first time in her life, *she had come home to herself, too.*

AUTHOR'S REFLECTION: WHEN YOUR BECOMING FINALLY MEETS YOUR BELIEVING

There's something sacred about the moment life begins to make sense; not because everything has fallen perfectly into place, but because *you* finally have.

I used to think alignment would arrive with pomp and circumstance, like I'd wake up one morning to confetti falling from the ceiling and a neon sign from heaven saying, "Now. Go do the thing you were born to do."

But the truth is, it is much quieter than that.

Gentler.

More tender.

It sounds like a whisper inside your chest that refuses to be ignored any longer.

It feels like the exhale you didn't realize you'd been holding for years.

That is what Camryn found when she stepped into her new space: her sanctuary disguised as a modest building with creaking floors and sunlight that seemed to know her name.

And that is what I've learned too:

The moment things finally feel right rarely looks magical from the outside.

But inside?

It feels like resurrection.

When purpose meets readiness.

When courage meets clarity.

When the woman you have become finally aligns with the truth you've been carrying all along.

I used to be terrified of starting again.

I used to call it failure.

I used to call it instability.

I used to call it proof that maybe I truly wasn't "cut out" for the rooms that kept spitting me out.

Now I understand that every time I pivoted, I was not losing ground; I was reclaiming it.

I wasn't starting over.

I was *starting toward*.

Toward the work that called to my spirit.

Toward the vision, I kept pushing to "someday."

Toward the life that was waiting for me the moment I stopped performing and started listening.

There's a version of all of us who stayed in places too long because we confused loyalty with purpose.

Who ignored our intuition because we were afraid of disappointing people who were never responsible for our destiny in the first place.

Who dimmed our brilliance just to survive rooms we were meant to outgrow.

But here is what I know now, deep in my bones:

Alignment doesn't chase applause.

It chases truth.

And truth has a way of following you around until you finally stop running.

When something is right, you don't have to twist yourself to fit it.

You don't have to translate your heart into something palatable.

You don't have to negotiate your identity just to belong.

You don't have to barter your peace for a paycheck.

Your becoming feels like home; soft, lived-in, familiar, even if you've never been there before.

And when you arrive in that space...

Even if it's small, even if it's humble, even if it looks nothing like what you imagined, there is an unshakable knowing that settles in your body:

This is mine.

This is me.

This is the work that God carved out with my name etched in the blueprint.

No title compares to that feeling.

No external validation can replace it.

No salary that can counterfeit the fullness of it.

Purpose has a sound: quiet, steady, ancient.

Purpose has a temperature: warm, grounding, familiar like sunlight on bare skin.

Purpose has a scent: something like eucalyptus, hope, and the courage to try again.

Purpose has a weight: never heavy, only whole.

And when you are aligned, the world does not get easier, *you* get clearer.

You stop begging for permission.

You stop auditioning for belonging.

You stop shrinking for comfort.

You stop apologizing for the woman you were always supposed to become.

So, if you find yourself standing in front of a door you prayed for, hand trembling, heart racing, unsure if you're ready, hear me clearly:

Turn the key.

Don't wait for confidence to show up before you move.

Confidence is not the prerequisite; obedience is.

Step into the room.

Let your purpose breathe.

Let your calling echo.

Let your courage speak up.

Let your spirit unfold in the newness of a life that finally fits.

And as you do, remember this truth:

You are not late. You are not behind. You are not unqualified.

You are right on time for the version of you that finally believes she deserves to take up space.

This is your moment.

Not because it looks perfect, but because you are finally whole enough to recognize it.

If Camryn's journey teaches us anything, it's this:

You don't need a bigger room.

You need a truer one.

You need a room where your brilliance doesn't need translation.

Where your softness isn't mistaken for weakness.

Where your truth doesn't require shrinking.

Where your presence isn't treated like an inconvenience but a gift.

And when you find that space, or build it yourself, something shifts in your spirit forever.

You stop merely surviving your life.

You start living it.

Fully.

Freely.

Finally.

This is the ending of the chapter, yes.

But it is also the beginning of the story you write next.

The one only you can tell.

The one you have been preparing for with every decision, every detour, every quiet act of courage.

Let this be your reminder:

When it finally feels right, you'll know.

And when you know, step boldly.

The life aligned with your purpose is waiting on the other side of your yes.

REFLECTION & DISCUSSION PROMPTS

What kind of work feels most aligned with your personal mission, and what would it look like to pursue it boldly?

What old versions of success do you need to release in order to build something new?

How do you want people to *feel* in the spaces you create?

What part of your story (your struggle, your wisdom, your becoming) are you finally ready to lead from?

_____

_____

_____

_____

CLOSING: BECOMING NEVER ENDS

There's something I need you to know:

I'm still becoming.

Even after the stages, the titles, the accolades.

Even after the healing, the clarity, the breakthroughs.

Even after the fear got quieter and my voice got stronger,

I am still learning.

Still shedding. Still rising.

And so are you.

Becoming isn't a destination.

It's not a checklist.

It's not something you graduate from.

It's a rhythm.

A return.

A reclamation.

You'll have days when you feel unstoppable.

And days when you feel like disappearing.

You'll have seasons where the world sees your glow, and seasons where you're growing in the dark.

Honor them all.

I hope you return to this book, not as a rulebook, but as a reminder:

A reminder of who you are when you're not trying to impress anyone.

Of what you carry when the world tells you to shrink.

Of how far you've come, even if your voice still trembles sometimes.

You're not broken. You're breaking open.

You are not behind. You are becoming.

You are not too much. You are exactly enough.

So keep showing up.

Keep choosing yourself.

Keep becoming, over and over again.

Because we need you.

We've always needed you.

And I'll be here… becoming, too.

With reverence and love, **Brandiss**

www.ingramcontent.com/pod-product-compliance
Lightning Source LLC
Chambersburg PA
CBHW060436130626
46555CB00005B/2388